OFFICE IDIOTS

What to Do When Your Workplace Is a Jerkplace

By Ken Lloyd, PhD

CAREER
PRESS

Pompton Plains, NJ

OFFICE IDIOTS

EDITED BY KIRSTEN DALLEY

TYPESET BY DIANA GHAZZAWI

Cover design by Howard Grossman
Printed in the U.S.A.

To order this title, please call toll-free 1-800-CAREER-1 (NJ and Canada: 201-848-0310) to order using VISA or MasterCard, or for further information on books from Career Press.

The Career Press, Inc.
220 West Parkway, Unit 12
Pompton Plains, NJ 07444
www.careerpress.com

Library of Congress Cataloging-in-Publication Data
Lloyd, Kenneth L.
    Office idiots : what to do when your workplace is a jerkplace / by Ken Lloyd, PhD.
        pages cm
    Includes index.
    ISBN 978-1-60163-268-5 -- ISBN 978-1-60163-525-9 (ebook)
      1. Problem employees. 2. Interpersonal relations. I. Title.

HF5549.5.E42L583 2013
650.1'3--dc23

                                                              2013012531

OFFICE IDIOTS

To my growing family.

ACKNOWLEDGMENTS

This book is based on e-mail that readers have been sending to my Website, *www.jerksatwork.com*, and to my weekly workplace advice column that has been running in several newspapers for more than 15 years. With that in mind, I offer major thanks to the many readers who took the time to write to me regarding some of the issues, concerns, problems, and, yes, office idiots they were encountering in their work. To all of these readers, I offer sincere thanks for their confidence and candor in expressing what's really going on in so many workplaces today.

And speaking of newspapers, I also offer great thanks to the outstanding team at the *Los Angeles Daily News* for their enduring support of my column over all of these years. Thanks also to the Los Angeles Newspaper group for running my column in some of their excellent newspapers. Special kudos go to three outstanding newspaper professionals who have played a key role in the success of my column: Greg Wilcox, Barbara Jones, and Kevin Smith.

Thanks once again to Career Press. This is my sixth book with this outstanding publisher, and I have consistently enjoyed working with their highly professional team. In this regard, I offer special thanks to Ron Fry,

Adam Schwartz, Michael Pye, Laura Kelly-Pye, Gina Talucci, Kirsten Dalley, and Diana Ghazzawi.

And finally, thanks also to my home team, composed of my amazing children and son-in-law, and especially to Roberta Winston Lloyd, a great librarian, researcher, editor, best friend, and wife.

CONTENTS

1

INTRODUCTION

Many books approach the subject of absurd, ridiculous, and outrageous workplace behaviors from the standpoint of hypotheses, anecdotes, and hearsay. The result is a combination of speculation and conjecture about idiotic workplace behaviors and what to do about them. This book is different. It's based on real incidents caused by real idiots in real workplaces. As well, the action steps to deal with them move out of the realm of guesswork and into the realm of real work.

An ongoing stream of e-mail to my newspaper column and Website keeps returning to one overriding theme: today's workplaces continue to be infested with office idiots. You would think that the recent economic slowdown would have pruned their presence to little more than a pesky weed here and there in most organizations. Or perhaps the jittery economy and current hints of recovery have somehow reenergized, refocused, and redirected the cadres of practicing office idiots.

Unfortunately, this isn't the case.

Office idiots can be found running companies and managing departments, and they're just as likely to function (or malfunction) as colleagues, peers, associates, fellow employees, or subordinates. You can even find them at the door in the form of job applicants. Their antics cover a vast spectrum of clueless, misguided, counterproductive, and downright inappropriate be-haviors. And when left unchecked, they're not only an annoyance, disruption, and distraction, they're a significant source of performance and productivity issues, as well.

So, herein you will find examples of some of the most widespread and dis-ruptive forms of office idiocy, along with a full toolset with which to deal with them. This not only means the optimum strategies for working over, under, around, beside, with, without, and in spite of office idiots, but also the strate-gies to rein in their idiocy. It's a compendium of what to say, what to do, and how to do it. And if you happen to possess any latent idiotic tendencies your-self, or if any such tendencies have somehow crept into your day-to-day work-place behaviors, this book shows you how to recognize and get rid of them.

As a side note, this book also uncovers the ways in which any of us can inadvertently enable and even reinforce idiotic workplace behaviors, thereby turning potential idiots into the real deal. There are enough idiots in most workplaces already, and there's no reason to engage in behaviors that create a corporate Petri dish that fosters their growth and proliferation.

What can be done about the infestation of office idiots that continues to turn any workplace into a jerkplace? The answer is in your hands.

1

OFFICE IDIOTS AND THEIR MISCOMMUNICATION

Office idiots distinguish themselves across a broad spectrum of absurd workplace behaviors, antics, and gaffes. One area that typically jumps to the front of the pack is their unique ability to easily and handily transform communication into miscommunication. Whether they're doing this on a witting, unwitting, or half-witting basis, the outcome is always the same: When office idiots insert themselves into the communication process, messages get mixed, muddled, and mangled.

Multitasking Mismanagement

In workplaces across America today, one commonly echoed complaint is that armies of idiotic managers are multitasking when their employees are trying to have a conversation with them. These managers pretend to listen and even occasionally react with an "Uh-huh" or an arched eyebrow, but they're actually hearing nothing.

For example, let's say you're discussing a matter of importance with your manager, but he's on his Bluetooth, glancing at his computer, pecking at the keyboard, and texting. You could tell him that the building's on fire, but he would probably either ignore it or ask you who's being fired. Importantly, if you keep talking as if he were actually listening, or if you pause here or there while he's focused on his other activities, you'll be wasting your time. Although you may be able to deliver your message, he's not going to receive it.

When your manager focuses on everything but you in a meeting, there are a few steps that can bring things back into focus. One way to deal with this brand of idiocy is by using the indirect approach. When he's no longer paying attention, ask him, "Is this a good time to meet, or should we get together later?" This question respectfully indicates that you recognize how busy he is, while still emphasizing that you need to meet. Depending upon your relationship with him, you can also use a more direct approach and say, "Hey, this is really important, and we need to talk. Can you put all that stuff down?" This type of approach includes an attention-grabbing opener, followed by a collaborative message that both of you need to go over something. By opening with "Hey," you're more likely to get him to look up at you. This break in his focus will help him hear your next words, namely that you need to meet.

And by the way, one of the most powerful and emotionally charged, attention-grabbing word to use right at the outset is someone's name.

Another useful strategy is to determine the time or times of day when he's least likely to be interrupted, and then set your meetings during those periods. Also, if you meet in his office, suggest that he sit down face-to-face with you, rather than from behind his desk. You can also propose a change in venues, for example, by suggesting that you meet in a conference room or at his coffee table if there's one in his office. The idea is to separate him from his distractions.

No Feedback

Another common variety of office idiocy in the arena of communications is the tendency of some managers to fail to provide feedback regarding messages or work submitted by their employees, especially when it's transmitted via e-mail. These communiqués and submissions simply tumble into the abyss of managerial idiocy.

Take the case in which it's the weekend and your manager sends an e-mail asking you to write up a description of a situation that occurred when she was away on business. You spend a couple of hours writing a summary, send it to her, and—nothing. You never hear anything back. Not one word. You're probably thinking that some thanks would have been nice, and some feedback wouldn't have hurt, either. After all, you went out of your way to work on this project, and a response is definitely warranted, whether it's a brief thanks or a couple of follow-up comments or questions. Your manager ignores this fact and ignores you.

■——————————————————————

There's nothing wrong with asking for her thoughts regarding the work you sent, provided that you don't sound like you're begging, needy, or fishing for compliments. In other words, avoid sending a message that basically says *I worked hard on that project, especially over the weekend, and I hope you thought it was okay.* In addition, you shouldn't call a meeting for the sole purpose of asking her what she thought about your work. If the matter at hand is so important, it's up to her to make it the centerpiece of a meeting.

A more productive approach is for you to mention it to her in passing, perhaps as part of another conversation or meeting, such as by saying, "How'd that write-up work for you?" This is an open-ended question that requires something other than a yes or no response, and it sets the stage for her to give you some feedback, and appreciation, if warranted.

Because your manager has demonstrated her skills in requiring employees to do extra work and then saying nothing in return, you should develop a strategy to prevent this from happening in the future. For example, the next time you complete a similar project for her, wrap up your e-mail with a question, such as, "What do you think of this approach?" or "Your thoughts?" Concluding with a question is certainly not needy, but it does need a response.

Read Before You Leap

While it's clearly annoying when an office idiot fails to provide any kind of response to a time-consuming project completed by her employee, there can be more than a modicum of annoyance when an equally idiotic manager provides a ridiculous response to such a project.

Let's look at a situation in which your manager asks you to provide status updates on various developments in your department. You respond with a very thorough analysis that includes considerable detail on the background, current status, and projections, and you spell out a specific series of steps that need to be taken. You're feeling good about your work on this one. After your manager receives your updates, he calls you to discuss. You're ready for a first-rate discussion. However, that balloon bursts when your manager starts asking some very basic questions. In less than a nanosecond, you realize that he never read what you wrote. He's obviously winging it. While he may have a perfectly good excuse for failing to read what you sent, there's no excuse for pretending that he did. All he should say is that he hasn't read it yet. Unfortunately, such candor and honesty are often well beyond the grasp of office idiots.

In response, you can say something charitable, such as, "If you need more time to go over this, we can discuss it later." However, most office idiots in this situation would rather have you tell them what you wrote. One of their common blowhard rationalizations will sound something like, "Well, as long as we've started, let's keep talking"—or, in translation, "I didn't read it before, and I'm not going to read it now." Ergo, the best you can do with this kind idiocy is to focus on increasing the likelihood that he'll read your work in the future. One key way to make this happen is to tailor the way you write to the way he reads.

Some managers—not yours, obviously—want to know every detail in the reports or analyses prepared by their employees. These managers often prefer carefully crafted paragraphs or extensive charts and tables that allow them to feast on numbers, metrics, and diagrams. Toward the other end of the continuum are managers who prefer reports that cut to the chase. These are the ones who like to read an executive summary, perhaps supported by some bullet points, but not much more. You need to determine where your manager "lies" on this continuum (and yes, the double entendre is intended). By chatting with him, looking at feedback he may have provided on previous reports that you wrote, and simply by asking him about his preferences in this area, you'll get a much clearer picture of what he likes to read and how you should write. Of course, depending on the degree of his office idiocy, you still may end up having to hold his hand and walk him through your work.

From Write to Wrong

While these two glaring and blaring signs of office idiocy—a manager's failure to respond to an employee's completed projects, or a failure to review a project and then fake it—are obvious, there's yet another idiotic step that many managers take in response to written work from their employees: They rewrite it. This is not necessarily a problem in and of itself. The real idiocy occurs when this rewriting turns the employee's original submission into an error-filled syntactical scrapheap.

Let's say your responsibilities include writing memos and updates, an area in which you're strong. Part of the process includes your manager reading your work before it's sent anywhere. So far, this isn't a problem. However, he makes changes that are grammatically incorrect, to the point that some of the information in the document ends up being indecipherable, incorrect, or both. Not surprisingly, when you show him the problems, he doesn't care. After all, what office idiot would? In fact, he insists that you send the messages *with his exact changes*. Among other outcomes, you end up looking incompetent, and you're also subjected to a barrage of flack from your fellow employees.

The irony in this situation is that if you refuse to follow your manager's directives, you may be written up (even though such a write-up will most likely be grammatically incorrect and unintelligible). Clearly you need to talk to him, in spite of the fact that he ignored you on the first round.

When you next meet with him, don't bother focusing on the problems associated with his writing, as that strategy won't register with him. Rather, take an approach that lets him see what's in this for him. For example, ask him, "If I came up with a way to save hours of your time every week, would you be interested?" This question should automatically elicit a yes, one of the most powerful words in the persuasive process.

With this positive context in place, tell him, "I can save you at least X hours every week if we go with my writing on these memos and updates. I've got the time. The employees are all for it. And this will free you up to work on the more important stuff." Then stop talking. (By the way, notice your subtle compliment indicating that he handles higher-level chores while you, his underling, will take care of this lesser task.) He may go along with your suggestion, or he may balk. If he opts for the latter, you'd go to Plan B, namely, the trial basis. This means you'd say, "Okay, I understand. How about if we go with my writing for a couple of weeks? If there are no problems, we'll stick with it. And if you're not happy, we'll look at some other approaches." Most people are willing to try almost anything for a stipulated short period that implies no commitment.

At the same time, note that you don't say that if this approach doesn't work, you will go back to the old approach of having him rewrite your work. Rather, all you say is that both of you will explore other options.

If he agrees to a trial period, you'll need to do everything in your power to make it work. And if this approach is successful, be sure to provide your manager with plenty of feedback, with most of the credit going to him. Most people appreciate recognition; if you provide it to him in relation to this project, he's likely to enjoy it and look for more. And that should further help extricate him from the role of would-be editor.

————————————————————————————■

Nonstop Questions

As part of the communication process, it's important for a manager to encourage employees to ask questions, and it's equally important for a manager to actually answer them. After all, there's plenty of evidence to indicate that managerial accessibility and responsiveness have a positive impact on employee performance, productivity, and morale. However, while there's no question that this kind of open communication is important, what about the common scenario in which an employee asks too many questions?

For example, let's say you're a manager, and you encourage your employees to "ask if they don't know." However, you have one employee who doesn't know when to stop. She keeps pestering you with questions, occasionally on topics that are, frankly, none of her business. Naturally, you don't want to discourage questions, but you also don't want to waste your time dealing with an endless onslaught of inquiries. The problem is that some office idiots are more interested in asking questions than in hearing answers. This questionable behavior gives them an extra opportunity to talk and be heard, and it even provides them with elements of influence, power, and control over their managers.

As the manager, it's up to you to determine when an employee's questions have crossed the line and moved into the realm of office idiocy. While there's no magic number that lights up after a specific number of questions, you'll know when it happens. It's the point at which you find that you've stopped listening to the questions and started asking yourself how you can get away.

With an employee who dishes out more questions than a game-show host, the first question to ask yourself is if you're too accessible to her. She obviously has a need to engage you in her questioning quest, and as long as you go along with it and provide answer after answer, she's going to repeat this behavior. After all, behaviors that are rewarded are repeated, and the time you spend with her is simply a big reinforcement pellet.

When her interminable line of questioning crosses the line, there are a couple of strategies that can help. First, depending upon the questions themselves, one approach is to encourage her to find the answers on her own by saying, "I'm interested in having you come up with an answer on this." The big advantage of this approach is that it stops her question in its tracks. Most employees don't like to tell their manager that they're incapable of doing what is asked of them. Furthermore, your response isn't derogatory, insulting, or dismissive; in fact, it implies that you have confidence in her ability to do some homework and find the answers she needs. When she finds that she keeps getting sent off to find her own answers to her questions, she's going to be less likely to ask them in the first place.

If her brand of idiocy requires a more direct approach, you can say something like, "I can't provide you with any more information on this matter," and then simply stop talking. The more often you use this approach, the less rewarding her questioning becomes. When she realizes that she's hit the limit that you've established, she'll be more likely to limit her questioning.

A Matter of Chatter

Then there's the flip side of the employee who asks nonstop questions: the employee who provides long, drawn-out answers to *your* questions. Even when you ask the most basic question, this office idiot comes back with a long-winded answer. On the one hand, you don't want to be rude and interrupt, but at the same time, you have other things to do besides listen to an endless flow of banal blather.

When every question you pose to an employee elicits a long-winded answer, there are some strategies to help temper the verbal tempest. First, there's the preventive strategy. Before asking her a question, ask yourself a couple of questions, such as, *Do I really need to ask her about this?* and *Is there a better person to ask?* In many cases, the best way to avoid her long answers is to avoid asking her any questions in the first place. If your response is that you still need to pose a question to this employee, set the stage before asking. For example, preface your question with, "I don't have much time, so I just need a brief answer."

If this employee still flips into endless answer mode, wait until she takes a breath and then interject a comment. People who are non-stop talkers are used to being interrupted, so they typically don't take much offense to it. When there's a break in the verbal action, jump in and say, "I really don't need that much detail." At the same time, on those occasions when she does cut to the chase, be sure to provide her with positive feedback for doing so, even something as basic as, "That's a great, to-the-point answer." When she receives positive reinforcement for keeping her comments brief, she's more likely to repeat this behavior, rather than repeat herself.

Holding Back Information

At the opposite end of the continuum of the office idiot who has no unexpressed thoughts is the office idiot who withholds far too much information when queried by his or her manager. One rule of thumb to keep in mind in this situation is that whatever an employee fails to tell you is never good news. After all, if the news is positive, he or she will voice it.

One of the more common forms of this withholding occurs when a manager asks an employee for an update on a given project, and the employee responds with a few cursory comments and nothing more. For example, take the scenario in which you've got an office idiot whose response to your inquiry regarding his progress is, "Don't worry." Of course, these are two of the most worrisome words an employee can say. When an employee uses this phrase, he's the one who has introduced the notion of worrying in the first place. Unfortunately, if an employee uses this expression, it's typically a sign that you should indeed worry.

In all but a very limited number of situations, when an employee is asked for specific information, a response of "Don't worry" is unacceptable. The amount of information to be provided is determined by you, not him. The next time you get this kind of a response from your employee, you should say, "I'm not worried. It's just that I need to see where things are with XYZ project, especially in terms of what's been done, where things are in terms of the schedule and deadline, and what the plan is going forward."

Your employee's response to this will tell you whether you really need to worry or not. If he gets a look of worry on his face, then it's time for you to worry, too.

At the same time, it should be noted that this phrase isn't an automatic red flag. There are managers who have worked with certain employees for years, and this phrase is taken to mean that everything is on schedule and will be done properly, just as it has in the past. Their common history has reduced the need for more extensive communication. Unless you have this type of history with your employee, he'll need to respond with some catchy information rather than a catchphrase.

W.H.A.T. Is With the Acronyms?

While acronyms can be a handy shorthand to economize on language and expedite communications, they can also be a royal headache when office idiots glom onto them and carry them to extremes. One of the more common examples of such idiocy is found in the companies that have acronyms for just about everything, but that do very little to let new employees know what they mean. Importantly, these are not common or widely used acronyms, such as snafu (shorthand for "situation normal, all [fouled] up"), but rather, internally developed acronyms that are only known by the employees themselves.

Take the case in which you've just joined a company and quickly find that you're lost in the land of acronyms. You're familiar with the standard acronyms in your field, but this company has many of their own, and no one has given you information about any of them. Obviously you don't want to keep asking what something means, but if you say nothing, you're lost.

Right from the start, it's ridiculous that the company hasn't taken formal steps to provide new hires with a complete listing of all of the commonly used, company-specific acronyms. This failure is either an indication of an exclusionary corporate culture that's unwelcoming to new employees, or it's simply a reflection of incompetency. Underlying either of these causal factors is plain old office idiocy.

If you're a new employee in such a company, you should ask questions whenever you hear an unfamiliar acronym, and you should do so ASAP. The first weeks on the job will set much of the tone and tenor of your tenure, and things will fare far worse if you're making mistakes as opposed to making progress.

In addition, when you learn the definition of an acronym, try to avoid asking about it a second time, even if that means making a note of it for future reference. Acronyms are part of what separates this company from others, and the sooner you pick up the lingo, the sooner you'll feel a part of the company rather than apart from it.

Further, if you've joined a company that's receptive to employee input, you should suggest that they develop a glossary for new hires and include it in the orientation materials. As a side note, when it comes to making this type of suggestion, you'll probably get a better hearing if you keep it short and sweet. In other words, use the KISS approach: "Keep it simple, stupid."

————————————————————————■

A Large Dose of Gossip

One of the more common office idiots that's found wandering around the halls, cube farms, and break rooms of corporate America is the gossip. This person thrives on gathering information, disinformation, and misinformation, and then distributing it to all interested and uninterested parties, in much the same way that a spreader distributes fertilizer on an open field. In many instances, the contents of both spreaders are strikingly similar.

The problem, of course, is what to do when you encounter the resident gossip. Let's take a situation in which you're working away and the office gossip approaches. He's always talking about what other people are doing or not doing, while simultaneously trying to pry information out of you. You've tried to get him to stop, and you've even told him that your manager has specifically said that he wants everyone to focus on work and *not* on gossip. In response, and as justification for his behavior, the local gossip counters by saying that he isn't gossiping because "what he's saying is the truth."

Not surprisingly, the gossiping employee is wrong on two counts. First, gossip is idle chatter about the affairs of other people, regardless of whether such drivel is fact or fiction. Second, your employee is wrong by acting in a way that contradicts your manager's directive. When employees immerse themselves in gossip, the outcome is a no-win situation. The company loses because time that should be spent on work-related matters is wasted or disrupted by inane conversations. In addition, gossip, whether accurate or inaccurate, can bring pain and stress to anyone whose name is included in the banter. Finally, being known as the company gossip, or even associating with this idiot, doesn't do much to enhance an employee's credibility, reputation, or career.

Rather than merely trying to stop the verbiage after it starts, you need to act more assertively and proactively. The next time he approaches you with one of his tales, say something like, "Look, I'm sorry, but I'm really busy." And then go right back to your work. By opening with an apology, you establish a nonconfrontational and nonjudgmental tone, which helps prevent the stronger words that follow from generating a defensive or aggressive response from him. And by saying you're busy, you're clearly implying that you're not interested.

If he still tries to spice up the story or interrogate you for tawdry tales, just keep doing your work. After a few seconds, it's time to use some nonverbal communication, such as raised eyebrows, shrugged shoulders, and open palms, which together suggest, "There's nothing more I can do about this." Soon enough, he'll take the hint and take his business elsewhere.

By depriving a gossip of his lifeblood—namely, information, stories, tales, and drama—while simultaneously making him feel ignored and unimportant, you're removing his most important reward. This may or may not stop him from gossiping, but it should stop him from including you in his gossip farm.

Spy and Spy Again

A twisted cousin of the gossip is the idiotic manager who's overly con-sumed with whatever it is that his employees might be discussing, whether it's personal matters, work-related issues, or even their opinion of the manager himself. He knows that the employees get quiet when he's around, and that just fuels his belief that they *must* be talking about him. In more than a few of these cases, some managers take an incredible leap of idiocy: They ask a selected employee to listen in on the others and report back to them.

Let's say that you're highly respected in your department, and many of your fellow employees share information with you regarding a broad spec-trum of work and non-work matters. One day, your manager calls you into his office, shuts the door, and asks you to keep an eye on things in the department and let him know what your coworkers are saying. If you're looking for just one piece of behavioral data to unequivocally prove that your manager is, in fact, a consummate office idiot, this is it.

First, it's unfair, unprofessional, unethical, and unacceptable for a man-ager to put an employee in this position. His action is guaranteed to create tension, conflict, and frustration for you, as well as interfere with all aspects of your work. By essentially asking you to choose between him and your cowork-ers, your manager is placing you in an untenable position. If you refuse to do this corporate dirty work, you'll alienate your manager; if you go along with his demands, you'll alienate your coworkers.

And don't think that your spying will go unnoticed by your fellow em-ployees. When your boss appears to know too much about them and their doings, they'll soon narrow down the source of the leak. At that point, your manager will have no use for you, and neither will your colleagues.

When your idiotic manager asks for your answer to this absurd request, one strategy is to reply, "We both have a ton of work to do, and I know an easier way to handle this." Then pause for an in-stant, which will pique his interest in what you're about to say next. "Everyone in our group is pretty talkative, and I'm sure they'd open up with you if they had the opportunity. You want to find out what's going on? Just talk with them."

One key aspect of this message is what isn't said. You're not saying no to your manager, nor are you degrading his patently ridiculous request. By avoiding a negative opening, you're also avoiding an argumentative response. You're actually opening with an undeniable statement regarding the amount of work awaiting both of you, a statement that generates an instant yes in his mind. By doing so, everything that follows will be framed in this context of agreement, thus making your next comment all the more palatable and persuasive.

By suggesting that he try communication instead of subterfuge, he knows that if he disagrees with you and refuses to talk to his own employees, he's going to look like an even bigger idiot. Thus, the stage is set for him to go along with your suggestion. And for you to go along without having to be a spy.

————————————————————————■

2

CONFLICT AND OFFICE IDIOTS

One of the most compelling characteristics of office idiots is their legendary ability to introduce and inflame conflict in any organization. And they certainly don't discriminate in terms of the types of people they draw into their embattled worlds. Office idiots are renowned for increasing frustration, complaints, and blood pressure for management, peers, subordinates, and anyone else who has the misfortune of wandering onto their battlefield.

The Conclusion Jumper

One of the most common ways that office idiots make conflict a way of corporate life is their uncanny ability to jump to conclusions, connect dots that are unrelated, and instantly flip into accusatory mode. Their tendency to draw twisted inferences from insignificant data creates a climate in which conflict is the norm.

For example, let's say you're a department manager who's been with your current employer for several years. Having been in your field for quite a while, it isn't surprising that you have a vast network of colleagues and contacts across your industry. Because you know and are known by so many people in your field, you receive calls every couple of weeks from recruiters to see if you'd like to change jobs. At this point in the game, you've been telling all of them that you're not interested. However, when you happen to mention these calls to your manager, he becomes upset. In a giant leap to an unfounded conclusion, he claims that you must be telling people that you're not happy here, and that's why you're getting these calls. In support of his warped reasoning, he cites the fact that he's happy with the company, and so he never gets such calls.

The reality of the situation is that you're being called by recruiters because you most likely have a solid reputation in your field. Recruiters call people like you for two reasons: one, they indeed would like to know if you're interested in changing jobs; and two, they would like to know if you're acquainted with anyone else who might fit the position(s) they're trying to fill.

Your manager has erroneously assumed that the reason for these calls is that you've put out the word that you want to make a change. Because he's woefully wrong about this, you should use a clear and businesslike approach: "I'm very happy working here and working for you. And if I were actually looking for a job, do you really think I'd tell you about these calls?" As he cogitates over this, you can add, "These calls are no big deal, and I'm not even close to interested in what these guys are offering."

And by the way, your manager's behavior raises serious questions about his leadership, interpersonal skills, and personal security. And that just might be the reason why he doesn't receive such calls. Ironically, if he now starts treating you poorly, you may end up having longer conversations with these recruiters.

The Warrior Boss

While the conclusion-jumping manager generates conflict in a somewhat circuitous manner, other managers are more direct, abrupt, and in-your-face. The most common example is the manager who prefers to make war rather than make nice. And on those rare occasions when he or she demonstrates a hint of kindness, that can be even scarier.

For example, let's say you have a manager who's insulting, unapproachable, and nasty, 24/7. Once in a great while, however, she can actually act like a normal human being. So, technically speaking, she's warlike only 23/7. And those rare moments of humanity can actually be more disconcerting than her normal bellicosity, because you're always waiting for the other shoe to drop.

In light of her battling behaviors, your *modus operandi* is to try to maintain just enough contact with her to get your job done, and not a shred more. You know exactly what you're dealing with when she's acting like an office idiot, and it's best to just stay out of her way. However, now you're concerned that she's in "human mode," but not just for an hour or two, but for more than a week—a record for her. What's going on? You're wondering if she's up to something, or if she's truly changed.

Of course, it's a shame that you automatically wonder if your manager is up to something simply because she's acting like a manager. On the one hand, it's possible that she's undergone a change and is becoming a kinder and gentler person. Perhaps she has experienced a major life change or made some adjustments in her medication or therapy. Maybe there's even a substance abuse issue that's under better control. On the other hand, she just might be a nasty person who, for some random reason, is having a good week. It's even possible that she's being kinder in order to cause you to drop your defenses so that she can have a clearer shot at you.

The best approach here is to deal guardedly with her, keep trying to do your best in carrying out your responsibilities, and give her short-term change more time. For better or for worse, you're likely to have your answer very soon.

Downright Insulting

Another patented strategy that office idiots use in order to convert conviviality into conflict is to launch an insult. And just to be sure that the insult is particularly egregious, office idiots routinely let the degrading words fly in front of an audience.

For example, you're sitting in a meeting, minding your own business and the business of the meeting, when your manager asks for suggestions on ways to handle a problem. After a few of your coworkers present their ideas, you decide to voice yours. Your manager, a classic office idiot, immediately laughs aloud and says he wonders how you could be so naïve. Naturally, you're embarrassed and upset, and these feelings don't dissipate overnight. In fact, even with the passage of several days, you're still likely to be burning as a result of this public scorching. One question that keeps running through your mind is whether you should say something to your manager about what happened.

Before jumping into the fray, let's start by affixing the proper moniker to this office idiot. He's a bully—a bully who's full of bull, in fact. If you're looking for classic bullying behaviors, he personifies a bunch of them by insulting, humiliating, and degrading employees, especially in front of others.

When faced with this type of idiocy, one perfectly acceptable approach is to ignore it. If a bully senses that you're not bothered by his antics, he won't get any gratification by bullying you. This won't change his personality, obviously, but it just might alter his behavior.

One likely outcome is that he'll look around and ply his bullying wares on someone else.

In terms of the bigger picture, remember that when a manager bursts into laughter at one of his employees, especially in a public forum, the most laughable thing in the room is the manager and his leadership skills (or lack thereof). This type of idiotic behavior has a measurably destructive impact on all of the attendees, especially in terms of their motivation, morale, commitment, and creativity.

Even if your suggestion was marginal, it still has the potential to serve as a springboard to new ideas and strategies to solve the problem at hand. By attacking you for your suggestion, your manager threw a major roadblock into the problem-solving process. In fact, it sounds like he may be more of a problem than whatever you and your associates were trying to solve in the first place.

If you don't want to ignore this idiotic bully, another option is to meet with him and voice your concerns in private. One problem is that although some bullies are all bluff and bravado, others are more than willing to engage in combat, especially when clashing with opponents who happen to report to them. Does this mean that you have to roll over when your idiotic manager plays the bully card? Not at all.

You can go with the classic assertive model, in which you describe what happened, tell him how you felt/feel, tell him how you'd like to be treated going forward, and then spell out some consequences if things don't change. With this approach, you'd say something like, "You know, when you laughed at my suggestion during the meeting, I ended up feeling really badly, and I don't think this did much for anyone else in the room, either. I'm mentioning this only because laughing at what we say, even if you're doing it in jest, ends up hurting everyone's morale, and I don't think anyone's going to voice a creative idea if they think they're going to get humiliated."

Or perhaps you're interested in an approach that's less direct but arguably more compelling, such as by asking, "I'm curious. What would you say to your manager if you were at a meeting and presented your thoughts, and then your manager laughed at you and called you naïve?" When he tells you what he would say to his manager, say just that to him. Notice that this approach isn't critical, threatening, or hostile. There's nothing about it that can raise his anger, defensiveness, or hostility. Rather, you're simply approaching him with a question that, if anything, implies that you value his opinion.

Depending on how things go, you may also want to use this opportunity to discuss your "naïve" suggestion, especially if you're able to demonstrate the ways that it can either solve the original problem or serve as a gateway to new and productive strategies to do so. If he somehow changes his opinion and decides to give your "naïve" idea a try, and if your idea just happens to work, you'll have the last laugh. But don't take it.

Put on the Spot

Another card that office idiots play in order to incite or maintain a high degree of conflict in an organization is to constantly put employees on the spot. The idea behind this pathetic game is to keep pushing an employee to the point that he or she is trapped, out of ammunition, and with no options other than to look foolish and capitulate.

Let's assume that you report to one of these card-carrying office idiots. Whenever you speak with him, whether it's in private, on the phone, or in public, you know he's going to dig into whatever you say until he can find a shortcoming, weakness, or hole in your logic. At that point, he's going to seize the opportunity and make you look like a fool, a weakling, or a lightweight at best.

He starts this game by asking you a question. If you answer it to his satisfaction, he keeps digging deeper and deeper, beyond the issue and even beyond your expertise and job responsibilities. Ultimately, you're pushed to the point where you sound like you don't know what you're talking about. At that point you're pinned, and he wins.

To make matters worse, you're likely to get that nervous, pit-of-the-stomach feeling whenever you need to speak with him, and that simply plays into his Machiavellian hands. When you show even a hint of nervousness, he sees it, seizes upon it, and keeps on drilling. You're fumbling. You're mumbling. Your stomach is rumbling. And that's exactly where this office idiot wants you.

You could let him know that his incessant questions, probes, and harangues are creating strong feelings of resentment, and not just for you, but for others as well. But how do you think he's going to react to that? Most likely, he's going to fire back with full force and engage in the very behaviors that you are trying to convince him to stop. Because this type of behavior is part of his personality and most likely reflective of his personal insecurity, self-doubt, and need to control every situation, you're not likely to say anything that will move him out of the world of idiocy and into the world of normalcy.

■———————————————

This situation is best addressed preemptively. Rather than putting yourself in a situation in which he can easily put you on the spot, a little prevention is likely to be the best antidote for his venomous antics. After all, although your manager is putting you on the spot, you've also been putting *yourself* in a difficult spot. You can easily and accurately predict your manager's behavior when you interact with him: No matter what you say or do, he drills down until he gets you to the point where you're confused, uninformed, and, ultimately embarrassed.

Because this aspect of your manager's behavior is so easy to predict, you can take proactive steps to deal with it. One such step is called the "what-if game." The idea is that prior to any interaction with him, you should come up with the most difficult questions that he could possibly ask, and then develop and even practice the best answers. As part of this approach, you might even want to ask some of your closer coworkers to help you determine the questions as well as the answers. If you're thoroughly prepared, you'll feel less nervous when you communicate with him, and your responses are more likely to accurately and effectively field his questions. He can go ahead and drill down, but that won't bother you because you already know the drill.

———————————————————————————■

As a side benefit, when he finds that he can't push you to the point of surrender, he isn't going to sense much satisfaction by incessantly badgering you. As a result, he's likely to take his "spot-on" behavior somewhere else.

Making Something Out of Nothing

There's also a school of office idiots that have particularly well-honed skills in transforming totally innocuous workplace situations and conversations into conflicts. Perhaps the most sinister aspect of this ploy is that these idiots use conflict as a diversion to deflect attention from their own inadequate or inappropriate behavior.

A typical example is a scenario where you're meeting with your manager and sitting across from him at his desk. The discussion is progressing satisfactorily until his phone rings. He answers it and starts babbling about some inconsequential matters for around 10 minutes. That's his first mistake. When the call ends, in true office idiot form, he goes right into attack mode, saying that you shouldn't try to read the papers on his desk when he's doing something else. Notice how this jerk says nothing about the inappropriateness of his taking a phone call; certainly, he proffers up nothing close to an apology for the interruption. Rather, he instantly brings up an entirely unrelated matter, seemingly out of left field. You're now in the position of having to defend yourself while he gets away with totally inappropriate behavior.

Had your manager been acting like a professional rather than a jerk, he could have prevented this situation in any number of ways, such as by blocking his calls while he was meeting with you, or telling you that he needs to take the call and continue the meeting later. He could also "man up" and apologize for taking the phone call. Further, if he is so concerned about confidential documents on his desk, he should turn them over or put them in his files. In addition to learning a little more about how to manage, this office idiot could apparently use some training in feng shui.

So, what should you say to him? The best option is to be assertive, look him in the eye, and say, "While you were on your 10-minute call, I was looking around, but not at your desk. I would never do that." Notice that you open your response with a pointed reference to his 10-minute call, subtly letting him know that the call was the problem, not you. No matter how he responds, stick with this type of answer.

Importantly, when you make your comments, speak in a normal voice and at a normal pace. While it may be tempting to slow down your speech and say each individual word clearly, distinctly, and forcefully, such a speech pattern is often a sign that a person is lying. In fact, don't be surprised to hear him use it when he responds to you. After you've said your piece and the meeting has wrapped up, you shouldn't bring up this matter again. In fact, the more you mention it, the guiltier you'll appear.

Looking further into the future, there are a few other strategies to consider. For example, if your manager frequently takes outside calls during meetings, bring some other work with you. If he gets a call, ask him if he would prefer to meet later. If he gestures for you to stay, move back from his desk and work on whatever it is you brought.

As a side note, the complaints that people voice about others often provide insight into their own questionable behaviors. You may want to keep that in mind the next time he shows up at your desk.

More Than Words Can Say

Just as your manager can stoke the coals of conflict, employees who report to you can easily do so, as well. While it makes little sense for employees to willfully generate conflict in dealings with their managers, employees who do so are office idiots, so this isn't really surprising.

One of the more prevalent examples of such idiocy is the employee who's constantly critical of her manager's performance and always ready for an argument or disagreement to prove a meaningless point. These employees often operate under the gross misconception that they're all-knowing, a delusion that's compounded by a lack of insight into the impact they have on others, total cluelessness in terms of the basics of human interaction, and complete ignorance of the nuances of manager-employee relations. With that foundation in place, they're a lit match in search of a bundle of potential conflict to ignite.

For example, let's look at a situation in which you have an employee who's overly critical of many of your decisions and actions. She's always ready to tell you that something you're doing is incorrect, outmoded, or outdated. And to make it worse, she uses a nasty tone, backed up by a perpetual scowl. This is an employee who's clearly in need of some feedback. In fact, until she's formally advised that her actions are inappropriate and unacceptable, she's going to continue to engage in them. If you say nothing, she's going to interpret your silence as tacit acceptance of her argumentative antics.

■———————————————————

Your first pass at feedback should come directly on the heels of these incidents of unacceptable behavior. For example, if she makes an inappropriate comment or gesture, or if her tone is mean, nasty, or condescending, tell her at that exact moment. The sooner that feedback is given after the behavior, the more compelling and effective it will be. Your comments should be clear, specific, and focused on her behavior, performance, and results—not on her personality.

For example, as soon as she flips into argument mode with you, stop the conversation and express your opinion and concern. If she's arguing when she should be listening, you should say something like, "I want to give you some feedback. I'm getting an argument with every point that I make, and I haven't even finished. It's okay to disagree with me. In fact, I encourage it. But it's not okay to constantly argue and fight and sneer, and that's what I'm seeing right now. What are we going to do about this?" Then stop talking and let her talk.

Ultimately, there'll be one of two possible outcomes. The first is that she'll get the message and try to give more thought to what she says and how she says it. The other is that she won't get the message and will continue to be a source of conflict for you and your department. In this case, she'll most likely need to be given another message, this time in writing. It would be a formal reprimand that spells out her inappropriate actions and indicates that she'll need to end them or be subject to more serious disciplinary action, up to and including termination. Upon receiving this type of notice, some employees shape up, while others ship out, either voluntarily or involuntarily.

―――――――――――――――――――――――――■

On the Defensive

While not as big of an office idiot as the non-stop arguer, the overly defensive employee is another common idiot that you may very well find within your ranks. In fact, you may have an entire platoon of such troopers. These employees function pleasantly and productively until they're asked why they took a particular action or engaged in a particular behavior, especially in situations that don't have a happy ending. Once this occurs, they bring the defenses out onto the field.

Let's take a case in which your team's project wraps up as a complete mess. You want to meet with the group to discuss what happened and figure out a strategy to prevent a repeat performance. The problem is that when you try to find out why things turned out so poorly, your employees become very defensive.

In this type of situation, there are a number of methods that can help keep employee defensiveness low and effectiveness high. The first is a preventative move meant to reduce the number of situations in which employees are making mistakes in the first place. In this regard, one of the best ways to prevent a project meltdown is to provide employees with frequent feedback, coaching, and guidance along the way, rather than after a project is completed.

When you discuss your employees' mistakes, you can reduce the likelihood of a defensive reaction not only by using the previously discussed strategy of focusing on performance rather than personality, but also by using a positive and constructive tone, along with more dialogue than monologue. Here's a helpful hint: when you're trying to determine why your employees took certain actions, it helps to avoid the word "why." This word has a scolding and parental tone that often leads to increased defensiveness. As an alternative, consider a more inquisitive and less confrontational approach, such as, "How is it that this was selected?" or "Can you tell me more about your thinking on that?" This type of wording elicits the same information as questions that start with "why," but without generating the defensiveness.

The Battle Zone

Beyond the individual office idiot whose calling card is conflict, there's a surprisingly large number of companies that have an entire culture of conflict, typified by widespread yelling and screaming. Office idiots in these organizations have no difficulty maxing out the decibels, totally unconcerned with the fact that their outspoken behavior is damaging, disgusting, and detrimental to the throngs of employees who prefer speaking over shrieking.

Let's take the case in which you're in an organization where yelling and screaming are everyday practices, while modulated and respectful conversations are regarded as weird and out of place. You're not a screamer, but you fear that if you don't turn every interaction into a shouting contest, you're going to be seen as weak, uncertain, and malleable, and the points you're trying to make will be overshadowed and then overlooked. Nonetheless, you don't want to succumb to this level of office idiocy, so you resolve to stay calm and steady when dealing with your outspoken associates. You hope they'll follow your example, but your ears are still ringing as a result of a recent discussion with your manager, and your head is a little achy after a so-called conversation with one of your coworkers.

One key takeaway in this situation is that when you repeatedly bang your head against the culture of a company, you're indeed likely to suffer, not only in terms of your performance, satisfaction, and personal morale, but also in terms of your physical health. It's particularly stressful for non-screamers to be in this type of setting, and it's not uncommon for them to experience such stress-related symptoms as headaches, backaches, ringing in the ears, high blood pressure, and eating and sleeping disorders. After all, it's virtually impossible for just one employee to change the corporate culture unless he or she is at the top. The problem is that your company's culture rewards employees who engage in behaviors that you're trying to eliminate, and the rewards from the company are greater than any rewards you can provide, so the thunderous behaviors prevail.

————————————————————————

The first point to recognize is that you can certainly try to remain calm in this turbulent environment, but you're not going to change it. In fact, your efforts to do so are likely to yield little more than frustration. Second, you need to decide if you really want to stay in a company that places a premium on behaviors that conflict with your style, values, and philosophy. When personal styles and values conflict with those of an organization, employees either change and become like the rest of the herd, or they change jobs.

Look around the company, especially at the people who are in positions that you aspire to hold one day. And then look at yourself. Is this where you really want to go? Is this what you want to become? As you answer these questions, there's one further point that's worth keeping in mind. If this climate of conflict is causing your health to suffer, that's a tip that should be the tipping point.

———————————————————————■

3

IDIOTIC JOB INTERVIEWERS

The job interviewing process is an arena in which some of the strangest, jerkiest, and most idiotic behaviors come into play—on both sides of the desk. On one side, we have the job interviewers. These screeners are supposed to be trained in the latest techniques, procedures, technologies, and legalities associated with hiring, but as job candidates across America have indicated, many interviewers are engaging in behaviors that are out-of-date, out-of-touch, and, in many cases, just plain outrageous.

Too Many Interviews

For example, imagine that you've just gone through four job interviews at the same company, and now you've been invited back for number five. You're assuming that they're interested in you, but you wonder how much longer this will go on, and you're seeking a way to get the company to give you an offer rather than another appointment. If you've been invited back for a fifth interview, the company is most likely very interested in you and in making the right hiring decision. With an extended screening process, the superficialities of initial job interviews are gone, and now you and the employer have a better opportunity to see if it's a good match.

Many employers today have the luxury of screening candidates at a glacial pace because the labor market for most jobs is flooded with applicants. However, when jobs are plentiful and applicants are scarce, employers that take extra time to screen applicants can easily end up losing the better ones.

At the end of the fifth interview, you should ask a couple of questions. The first should focus on what the next steps will be. For example, "I'm just curious...can you tell me about the timing of the process going forward?" Your second question should actually be a closing question, such as, "Is there anything else you need before making a hiring decision?" If the answer is no, you should sit and wait for the interviewer to speak next. If the answer is yes, you should find out exactly what it is, and then give him or her whatever is needed as soon as possible.

If you don't start asking some closing questions, you may find that the screening process isn't going to draw to a close anytime soon.

Summarily Rejected After Multiple Interviews

Then there's the other side of the extended screening process. Let's say you were interviewing for a management position, and everything seemed to be going well. You returned to the company on three separate occasions, and you were interviewed by several senior-level people. You felt that you aced the entire process, but were shocked to receive a two-line e-mail saying the position wasn't going to be filled and that the company was going in a different direction.

When a company tells you that it's "going in a different direction," your best step is to go in the *opposite* direction. After taking so much of your time and theirs, the company has made its decision. Granted, it would have been more professional if you had been informed of this fact with something more substantial than a two-line e-mail, but the fact is that you're not getting this job. If you want to contact the company to discuss the decision, that's literally and figuratively your call. But really, if they wanted to discuss things with you, they would have done so already. Two lines of e-mail to an applicant who has had multiple interviews doesn't say much about the company's character, credibility, or sense of goodwill. One might also wonder if they truly called off the search, or if they simply decided that it's easier (read: less messy) to reject a candidate by saying that no one was hired.

Again, in today's flooded labor market, some employers aren't treating candidates with the respect they deserve. When the labor market tightens up, these kinds of idiotic corporate antics will fall by the wayside. In the interim, you can make better use of your time by focusing on potential jobs rather than allegedly nonexistent jobs.

Extremely Brief Job Interviews

Rather than being called back for multiple interviews, in which there appears to be great interest in you and your career, many applicants are encountering the exact opposite—namely, a ridiculously abbreviated job interview.

For example, let's say you just had a job interview that lasted all of 10 minutes. The interviewer opened by saying he was very busy and then rushed through a few questions and summarily ended the "interview." You heard nothing from the company after that, and you're wondering what to do next. In reality, the office idiot who interviewed you should be a candidate for an exit interview. This type of treatment is unprofessional, unkind, and unacceptable. In the first place, an interview that lasts 10 minutes isn't an interview at all; it's little more than an introduction. Secondly, the lack of follow-up from the company, even if it's a rejection letter, further demonstrates a total lack of professionalism. If an interviewer is only able to conduct a ten-minute interview, the applicant should be advised of this as soon as possible, hopefully before he or she even arrives. But the fact is that such an interview shouldn't even be held at all. Either way, a follow-up interview should be scheduled. And if the interviewer becomes too busy because of a major last-minute development, he or she should apologize and reschedule.

——■

Assuming that you didn't do anything that would warrant such a short interview, such as destroying the furniture in the waiting area, you may want to send an e-mail to the interviewer's manager and/or to the HR (human resources) manager. If you really want to have some fun, send it to the president of the company. Such an e-mail should be very brief and to the point—for example: "I was interviewed by Mr. or Ms. X today for the position of such-and-such, and I thought you'd want to know the following...." At that point, use short sentences or bullet points to describe what happened. You can wrap up the e-mail by saying, "I was very disappointed with this treatment, and I am sure that it wasn't representative of the way in which your company treats job candidates, customers, or the general public."

You have absolutely nothing to lose by sending this type of message, and the response from the company will tell you if it's worth even a minute more of your time.

■——

The Waiting Game

In some cases, employers opt for a strategy that's arguably worse than the abbreviated interview: the non-interview. The candidate is ready and waiting to be interviewed, but because "things are running late," he or she is essentially placed in a holding pattern. At some point (usually later rather than sooner), the candidate is advised that extenuating circumstances have forced them to cancel the interview. It usually goes something like this: you go to a job interview that's scheduled for 9 a.m., and the receptionist tells you there's a slight delay. At 9:30 a.m., you approach her and request an update.

She calls someone and then says it'll be a few more minutes. At 10:30 a.m., you walk out. Odds are you'll never hear from the company or the person who was supposed to interview you, but you still may ask yourself if it was a mistake to walk out. When your scheduled job interview is one-and-a-half hours late, and there's no indicator that anything close to an interview is on the horizon, it's easy to understand why you'd opt to leave.

With no apology, no rescheduled appointment, and no follow-up communication, there's no pressing need to go any further with this employer. Nonetheless, with the company in the rearview mirror and no sign of anything ahead, you have nothing to lose by writing a businesslike letter to the HR manager and/or the president of the company and letting this person know how you were treated. By doing so, you'll find out if this incident is solely a reflection of the interviewer or of the company at large.

Importantly, corporate leaders today are realizing that this type of treatment can cost the company a great deal in terms of lost customers and damaged goodwill. After all, this morning's idiotic treatment of a job candidate just might end up on the candidate's Facebook page this afternoon, and who knows how far and wide it'll go from there? Hopefully, you won't encounter this type of treatment again in the future, but it isn't exactly a rarity in today's environment. If it *does* happen again, you should approach the receptionist and say, "Can you please check with the interviewer and see when we can schedule another appointment?" The answer to this question is actually going to answer several questions you likely already have about this company.

Bias Against Body Art

Now let's literally turn the tables and place you in the employer's chair as an interviewer. What are some of the more common idiotic behaviors that your manager and colleagues can exert as you try to screen applicants fairly, legally, and professionally?

Let's take the case in which you're about to start the interview process, but things don't actually begin with you. Rather, everything starts with the bias of your boss. For example, there's the surprisingly common situation in which a manager insists that interviewers ask candidates if they have any tattoos or piercings. He claims that such things show risk-taking and impulsiveness, and he doesn't want anyone with those characteristics in the department. You don't agree with his thinking, and you really don't want to ask candidates probing questions on this matter.

In terms of the bigger picture, hopefully your manager's understanding of managerial principles and practices is more current and accurate than his understanding of human behavior and ethical hiring practices. He's inappropriately fixated on what most consider to be an archaic stereotype, namely, that an applicant with a tattoo or piercing is somehow destined to be a wildly problematic employee.

———————————————

In the first place, you should mention to your manager that all pre-employment inquiries should be job related, and tattoo- or piercing-related questions are anything but that. A central problem is that it's impossible to accurately predict job performance on the basis of body art. There are great employees with tattoos, as well as terrible employees with tattoos. When the policy is that any tattoo or piercing means elimination from consideration for a job, the result is likely to be the loss of some good candidates, and possibly some legal exposure, as well. Further, asking this type of question can annoy a job seeker, to the point that some candidates will think twice about accepting your job offer if one is forthcoming. And if this type of questioning happens to cause individuals in protected categories to be eliminated at a disparate rate, the likelihood of legal problems is stepped up a notch.

It may be helpful to remind your manager that some applicants have body art in places that are not visible during the job interview, while other applicants are advised to cover their tattoos or leave their piercings at home until after they're hired. Now what are you supposed to ask? If your manager really wants to learn about an individual's qualifications and suitability for a given position, the best place to look is at the work history rather than the body art.

As a side note, your manager may be interested in knowing that eliminating job candidates on the basis of tattoos would have knocked out Winston Churchill, Theodore Roosevelt, Barry Goldwater, and Thomas Edison, just to name a few.

Hopping to Conclusions about Job-Hopping

Another common idiotic problem is caused by the various biases and stereotypes that exist regarding the issue of job stability. Take the case in which there's a need for an additional person in your department, and your manager asks you to help screen resumes. So far, so good. It's not a bad idea to solicit input from current employees regarding the candidates who are being considered to work alongside them in the future. However, your manager insists that any candidate who has had more than three jobs in the past two years must be eliminated from consideration. Period. You don't agree, and you've voiced your opinion about this standard, but she won't budge.

In reality, it's your manager's rule that should be eliminated, not these candidates. However, if you want to convince her that her standard is actually substandard, you'll need to do more than voice an opinion. Your manager needs to hear some facts.

For example, there are completely acceptable reasons for having more than three jobs in two years. In today's economy, there are lay-offs and company relocations, along with situations in which learning opportunities, supervisory practices, or ownership changes induce or force employees to make a switch. The fact that employees change jobs under these circumstances often has nothing to do with their performance, competence, loyalty, or commitment.

You should have no reluctance to let your manager see resumes of solid applicants who have made relatively frequent job changes in a short period of time. If you can include explanations for their transitions, so much the better. Your manager needs to understand that her arbitrary elimination of qualified candidates is doing a disservice to these applicants as well as to your company. Simply looking at the number of jobs an individual has held in two years is far less important than looking at the individual.

Pre-Employment Inquiries That Spell Trouble

Amazingly enough, there are still managers who ask totally inappropriate questions during the hiring process. One common finding is that some of these office idiots assume that they have a wild card if they preface such a question by saying, "I know I'm not supposed to ask questions in this area, but...." They then go on and ask ridiculous personal questions that clearly violate laws and statutes related to equal employment opportunity.

A related practice is when office idiots sneakily insert these kinds of questions in settings other than during the actual interview. For example, after you conduct interviews for an open position in your department, your manager likes to join you and spend a few minutes with you and the applicants. The problem is that he asks personal questions, such as by asking young women if they're married, if they have children, or if they're planning on having children. Perhaps you told him there are laws against these kinds of questions, but his reaction is that he's just having an informal chat with the applicants. After all, you already completed the formal interview.

Although it makes sense for you to be concerned about your manager's questions and voice your concerns to him, the issue that you're encountering is much broader. His line of questioning is the reflection of a value system in which he places himself above the law, above the concerns of his employees, and above the concerns of any applicants. This sends a terrible message about the company, and with today's social networks, that message can go far and wide very quickly and easily.

In dealing with your manager's idiocy in this area, it's critical to remember that you can't change his values, but if you're lucky, you *may* be able to change his behaviors. Start the process by saying a few precautionary words, such as, "We've really got to keep the questions focused on job-related topics. Personal questions can easily lead to lawsuits, especially in times when it's tough to find a job. And the judgments can be hundreds of thousands of dollars. And they don't do much for our company's image or goodwill either." Notice that this wording doesn't accuse your manager of wrongdoing, but simply provides the daunting facts. By using the words "we" and "our," you are taking a team-oriented approach and including the message for yourself as well as your manager. This further removes the sting from what you are saying.

If this doesn't work, you can add something like, "If you want more info on this, the best person to talk to is our company attorney." Besides, if he continues with his current line of questioning, that's exactly what he's going to be doing anyhow.

Some office idiots engage in a version of this line of questioning but refrain from doing so within the confines of the workplace. Instead, they go offsite.

For example, take the case in which you and two or three associates have completed your interviews with a strong candidate, and you decide to take him to lunch. During the meal, one of your idiotic associates launches a barrage of personal questions at the candidate, including queries about his family, religion, and roots. The applicant answers them, but looks a little shocked. After this unpalatable experience, you tell your colleague that these types of questions shouldn't be asked, and he tells you that since this was an informal lunch and not a real interview, he can ask whatever he wants.

The problem is that your colleague somehow thinks that when he's in a venue that includes silverware and a menu, he can order whatever he wants and therefore ask whatever he wants. However, he's literally and figuratively out to lunch on this one.

———————————————————————

Once again, it's essential to let your colleague know that all pre-employment questions, no matter where they are uttered, must be job related. With this approach, an employer stays within the established pre-employment guidelines while still learning a great deal about the suitability of an applicant for a given position in the company. A person's work history provides a great deal of insight into his or her motivations, energy level, persistence, work style, and expertise. With the addition of some work samples and job-knowledge questions, you can have a great discussion that sheds a tremendous amount of light on the applicant.

And by the way, it's equally important to remember that applicants are interviewing employers during the pre-employment process, too. When an applicant appears shocked by a line of questioning, it would not be shocking to find that he or she has taken his or her job search elsewhere.

———————————————————————

In Reference to Letters of Reference

Surprisingly, many employers today still somehow believe that letters of reference flashed by job applicants provide vital background information. The problem is that such endorsements are almost always positive, and they're very easy to fake.

Take the case in which your manager has just interviewed a job candidate and tells you that he thinks this individual is perfect for the job. When you ask about the candidate's references, your manager hands you copies of three letters that glowingly describe the candidate's work, character, and unbridled greatness. Your manager then states that these letters are so strong that no further references are needed.

———————————————

In reality, there are several points that your manager has overlooked and you might want to share with him. First, everything that this glib candidate says during the interview and writes on his resume could be bogus. Reference checks are actually reality checks, and they're a must for every candidate that a company is thinking of hiring.

It's easy and tempting for applicants to embellish their resumes with positions, titles, and degrees that they never held or earned. Some candidates are even advised to overstate their qualifications in order to stand out from the rest. Moreover, do you really think an applicant would ever show a potential employer a less-than-positive letter? Most references wouldn't even dare to write such a letter.

And just to taint the process even further, some of the glowing letters are fake from top to bottom, created solely by the candidates themselves. Although a job candidate may interview well, the sad truth is that the best con artists are articulate, charming, and highly persuasive. Even if a call to an applicant's references generates nothing more than validation of his or her employment dates and job title, at least you'll have verification of some of the information that the applicant provided.

And by the way, U.S. law stipulates that employers are required to only employ individuals who have a legal right to work in the United States. In order to operate in accordance with this requirement and maintain a legal workforce, applicants are required to provide a combination of several documents, such as a U.S. passport, a certificate of naturalization, a Social Security card, and various other documents, depending on the individual circumstances. Some companies are also using outside professional services to verify a candidate's legal right to work in the U.S.

If a job candidate contends that this standard is met by a sterling reference letter that speaks to his or her right to work in the United States, your manager may be impressed, but effective hiring requires verification rather than infatuation.

———————————————————————————■

4

IDIOTIC JOB APPLICANTS

Employers that engage in bizarre hiring practices and rituals are not the only idiots in the pre-employment process. You can easily find a vast array of idiots on the opposite side of the desk, as well. Although applicants are constantly advised to behave in ways that showcase their best qualities and characteristics, there are still cadres of candidates across all labor markets who either ignore this advice or are simply unaware of it. The result is a demonstration of idiotic behaviors that are guaranteed to keep job-seekers in the position of seeking jobs, rather than in the position they're seeking.

Talking vs. Stalking

On the one hand, it's important for job candidates to learn about the company where they are about to be interviewed. At the same time, candidates who go too far in the pursuit of such information can wander into a virtual quagmire, only to emerge with the label of "jerk" clearly stamped on them and their file. Because companies are not advertising for jerks, the outcome isn't likely to be positive.

By doing some homework and gathering basic information about a company, its products and marketplace, and related newsworthy developments, job candidates can demonstrate their interest in the company, motivation to obtain the job, and even their research and data-gathering skills. While the amassing of such information is a good idea, it becomes an idiotic idea when pushed to an extreme. In this regard, a growing number of candidates don't know where to draw the line.

Take the situation in which you're conducting a job interview, and the applicant blurts out a bunch of personal information about *your* schooling, hobbies, and family, all of which he found by digging around on the Internet. The applicant thought you'd be impressed with his interest and research skills, but you're not.

Although an applicant can easily turn a job interview into an exit interview by demonstrating little or no knowledge about a potential employer, the same outcome is likely to occur if the applicant goes too far in accumulating personal data about the interviewer. When candidates blurt out such information, interviewers are more likely to feel violated than impressed. Ultimately, candidates who go too far in this area don't go too far with the company.

A job applicant's knowledge about a company or interviewer should indicate that he or she is a highly interested and motivated job seeker, but not a stalker. As noted above, knowledgeable employers keep their pre-employment questions focused on job-related topics, and job candidates who are interested in avoiding the jerk label are well-advised to do likewise.

Whoever Blinks First

It's rather surprising to find that locking eyes with a job interviewer is becoming a more common practice. Perhaps today's applicants are trying to emulate the late Steve Jobs and his mesmerizing, intimidating practice of staring deeply into the eyes of others without blinking. In reality, these applicants are better advised to try to emulate some of Steve Jobs' other creative and brilliant practices, rather than his stirring stares. Such applicants need to remember that they're job candidates, not Jobs candidates.

What happens when you're interviewing a candidate who constantly stares into your eyes and hardly ever blinks? The most likely reactions are distraction, discomfort, and a generalized feeling that the applicant is either clueless or a bit weird. And going one step further, what do you do with a seemingly suitable candidate whose background and work experience for the open position look fairly good, but whose staring during the interview makes you wonder if he's worth considering any further?

Perhaps this applicant is trying to send a (not-so-subtle) message that he's honest. After all, there are still people who believe in the myth that dishonest people won't look you in the eye. Such true believers engage in excessive staring in order to telegraph their high degree of honesty. In all honesty, dishonest people are aware of this mythology, so they'll gladly look you in the eye. Although job applicants are indeed advised to look job interviewers in the eye, they're also told not to stare. They're typically told to make intermittent eye contact, and then shift their glance to something else.

If you have doubts about dismissing the candidate primarily because of this one little factor, one option is to bring him back for a second look. Literally. Importantly, such an interview should either be conducted by someone else or, as a joint interview, by you and another interviewer. Perhaps the candidate will have read up on job interviews in the interim and will have placed his practice of staring on a back burner. Or maybe the staring won't be as intense as it felt in the initial interview. Either way, when the interview is over, you and the second interviewer should discuss this candidate to determine if you see eye-to-eye on his suitability for employment with your company. With this approach, it'll be much easier for you to determine if you should keep an eye out for a better candidate.

Lying Their Way In

In today's flooded and highly competitive job market, growing numbers of applicants succumb to the temptation to embellish their resume beyond any standard of reasonableness or honesty. There are even "experts" who recommend nothing short of lying in order to make a resume stand out from the pack.

Let's say you've been trying to fill a particular position for several months, to no avail. Finally a candidate shows up who seems to be a perfect fit. She has experience, expertise, great communication skills, and even a college degree, although the position doesn't require one. As part of the screening process, you let her know that her employment is conditioned on a satisfactory background check. She signs the company's background release form, and you're feeling good about things—until the background report arrives. It indicates that your candidate does not have a college degree.

———

You shouldn't drop her on the spot, because there could be a mistake at the university or the screening company. Instead, ask her about it: "We did the background check, and it came back and said that you don't have a degree. What do you make of this?" In virtually every case, you're likely to hear something like, "Oh, you know, I was told if I really wanted to get a job, I should say I have a degree. I know it was wrong, but I'm only a couple of classes away, and the job doesn't require a degree."

The real issue is that although a given job may not require a degree, presumably it does require honesty. Embellishing a resume means adding some finer points or details that enhance the basic content. Falsely asserting that one has a degree moves out of the realm of embellishment and into the realm of deception.

If you somehow decide to hire this idiot, it's going to take a long time for you to trust her. A very long time. In the interim, you will likely watch her more carefully, question her work, and intentionally or unintentionally send her a message of distrust. At the same time, she's not going to be delighted by working in a company where she feels embarrassed, exposed, distrusted, and disrespected. These feelings can easily undermine her attitude, performance, and loyalty. As a result, you'd be well-advised to look for someone else. You've been searching for months already, so another month or two is not going to hurt. And it's certainly not going to hurt as much as making a bad hire. Besides, people who lie about their degrees and slip past the gatekeepers usually have one thing in common: they are far more likely to fail.

As a side note for those candidates who are a few classes short of a degree and thinking about conferring one on themselves, the best advice is to *get your degree*. A job is not nirvana when you obtain it under false pretenses.

The Phantom Job

Rather than grossly lying about degrees that they lack or jobs that didn't exist, some candidates who have been unemployed for extended periods of time are advised to take a softer approach and simply state on their resumes that they have been self-employed in "consulting" during this period. The problem with this common tactic, of course, is that although "consulting" may indeed look more impressive on a resume, this is nothing less than including fiction in a document that's supposed to be non-fiction. In other words, it's a lie.

This kind of blatant fabrication will almost certainly come to light as part of a background check, but it's also likely to become more than obvious during a job interview. Candidates who pretend they have been consultants are known to fumble and stumble when an interviewer asks them about their specific consulting projects, clients, or contacts in the client organizations.

When unemployment is high, vast numbers of outstanding candidates are out of work, many for extended periods of time. Most employers understand this fact, and the stigma that used to be associated with being out of work while searching for a job has all but disappeared. Thus, there's no need for, benefit in, or excuse for lying about being a consultant.

If you are thinking about falsely stating on your resume that you are a consultant, the best advice is to actually be one, such as by doing pro bono work for an organization that could use some help. This means that you'd truly be consulting, a fact that would help build your resume, sense of self-esteem, credibility, and network, not to mention the fact that it would do some good, as well. This step is also guaranteed to prevent the kinds of trust issues noted previously when candidates are hired under false pretenses and never quite get over them. It would also reduce the likelihood of job failure that haunts so many employees whose resumes stray far from reality.

Your Boss's Buddy

Another common problem arises when your manager tells you that he has a friend who'd be perfect for an open position you've been trying to fill. The problem is that your boss's buddy is an idiot.

Take the case in which you've been trying to find a number-two person in your department, and your manager refers his friend to you. You contact her and ask her to send in her resume. She says she doesn't have a current one but will put one together. Three days later you receive a half-completed resume that's almost useless. She says she didn't have time to finalize it but wanted to send what she had. Your manager is okay with this, but you're not.

One key concern right at the outset is that when people are in job-search mode, they typically do their best to sell themselves as well as their labor. If this incident is an illustration of this candidate's best work, it's a bright red flag. In light of the importance of submitting a first-rate resume, this person should have put in the time to create one, regardless of her other commitments. At the very least, she should have contacted you and requested an extension. When you see this type of behavior in the recruitment and screening process, you can easily hypothesize that this is likely to be the way she'll act as an employee.

Perhaps she's operating under the assumption that her friendship with your manager is all she needs to obtain this job. Obviously she's wrong, and you should speak to your manager about this. You could say something like, "I know you're interested in having us hire so-and-so for this position, but I'd like you to take a look at her resume." At that point, hand your manager a copy of the resume and say nothing. Notice that your opening comment is a factual statement that can only generate agreement, followed by a request. You're not using any disparaging adjectives to describe the candidate or her resume; you're simply asking for your manager's views on her work. By doing so, you're automatically implying respect for his judgment.

And now it's her resume that's doing the talking. If it's truly shoddy, sloppy, and semi-complete, your manager will be more likely to reconsider the halo that he has placed over his friend. As he reads through it, you can then say something like, "I'm concerned that the way she approached this resume is the way she'll approach the job, and we can't afford that. If she sends an updated resume in the next day or two, we can reconsider. But if this is it, I think we can do better."

By saying that you think "we can do better," you are sending two key messages to your manager: first, the word "we" indicates that you are aligned with him in this hiring process; second, it's tough for a manager to disagree with an employee whose primary interest is to raise the bar and maintain high standards.

As a side note, hopefully his friend will learn that a half-completed resume is going to cut the likelihood of a job offer in half.

Drawing a Blank

As part of the pre-employment screening process, many employers ask job candidates to complete an application blank. Surprisingly, some candidates show varying degrees of resistance to this request. One of the most common forms of such resistance occurs when the candidate simply writes "See resume" all over the form.

Even more surprising, when hiring managers go back to such candidates and ask them to complete the entire application blank, a significant number still show passive and even active resistance. One of the most common behaviors is to race through the form, thereby creating an incomplete, inaccurate, and sloppy piece of career clutter. This is certainly an idiotic way to attempt to impress a potential employer, and yet many employers are uncertain when it comes to interpreting this type of behavior.

■————————————————

Completing an application blank is the first real assignment that you're giving to job candidates. With that in mind, here's the important question: How do they handle it? Do they approach this project carefully and do a thorough job, or do they show disinterest, resistance, or nonchalance? Based on the candidate's handling of the application, what can you conclude about his or her energy, drive, persistence, and interest in the job?

A big advantage to using the application blank is that it levels the playing field. Although it can be difficult to compare one resume to another, primarily because the candidate only tells you what he or she wants you to know, an application blank puts all of the candidates literally on the same page. In addition, an application blank provides information regarding the candidate's likes and dislikes on the job, reasons for changing jobs, and salary progression, all of which are typically omitted from resumes.

In addition, the actual appearance of the application blank can be very revealing. For example, the fact that a candidate's application blank is thorough or vague, sloppy or detailed, complete or incomplete provides valuable insights into his or her motivations, drive, and work style. When a candidate begrudgingly or half-heartedly completes an application blank, that speaks much louder and more accurately than his or her resume.

With all of this in mind, if an applicant gives the application blank short shrift, that is exactly what you should give the applicant.

Covering Too Much in Cover Letters

A cover letter can be an important component in the job search process, but a large number of candidates today are operating under the misguided assumption that if a one-page cover letter is good, a longer cover letter is great.

Take the case of a job candidate whose resume isn't very strong, especially since he changed lines of work several times in recent years. One potentially productive way to deal with this rocky career path is to provide a compelling explanation in a cover letter. The problem is that all of the explanations can easily lead to a cover letter that's two or three pages long. And for better or for worse, the sheer length of these letters says more than their words.

To avoid instant classification as an idiot, a candidate's cover letter should be a compelling introduction that entices an employer to read his or her resume, while providing information and details that are not typically on a resume. Such information can include the rationale behind job changes, his date of availability, and his willingness to relocate if the position is in a different geographical area from his current locale.

Although there's no hard and fast rule, a cover letter typically shouldn't exceed one page, and it definitely shouldn't be longer than a person's resume. When a screener opens a cover letter and sees a multi-page document, it can lead to several negative conclusions about the candidate, even before a word is read. For example, the candidate can easily appear to be covering for career deficiencies, ill-informed about the hiring process, or unable to get to the point, none of which are highly sought-after qualities in new hires.

If you're looking for a job and want to be seen as a viable candidate rather than a veritable idiot, keep your cover letter to one page and use it primarily to provide the kind of information noted above. Frankly, employers are more interested in seeing a candidate's actual work history than seeing a lengthy narrative that attempts to rationalize or explain it. The idea is to let your cover letter set the stage, while letting your resume play the starring role.

Information Overload

A quirky relative of the exceedingly long cover letter is the outrageously long resume. In spite of widespread advice to the contrary, large numbers of job candidates feel compelled to fill their resumes with every conceivable and inconceivable piece of minutia from every job they've ever had, including their current one. If the goal of this approach is to impress a potential employer, it's nothing more than a fool's goal. What is even more amazing is that some candidates will not only opt for the extra-long resume, but will package it with an extra-long cover letter and other extraneous materials as well.

Take the case in which a candidate responds to your online ad with a 12-page resume, a four-page cover letter, and five reference letters. The most common outcome is that before reading one word, you're likely to react negatively to the applicant because of this over-the-top response. With this massive data dump in hand, it wouldn't be surprising to find that you are left with but one question: Does this type of massive outpouring of data tell you all that you need to know about the applicant?

While it's tempting to simply take this overly verbose job candidate out of the running, there are still a few points to keep in mind before moving on to the next candidate. Rather than giving you specific facts about this candidate, his outpouring of information generates little more than conjecture. In this regard, such a response pattern indicates that a candidate may be either thorough, detail-oriented, compulsive, desperate, dependent, or even uninformed about the process of finding a job.

Because this candidate's materials can be interpreted in so many different ways, you should at least take a look at them. This doesn't mean that you need to spend hours mulling through this mountainous terrain of verbiage, but a little speed-reading will definitely help. After all, there are some specialties in which voluminous resumes are practically an industry standard, such as in the IT field.

The idea is to give the submission a quick overview while keeping an eye out for key words that match the position you're trying to fill. For example, depending on the position, you may want to look for words or terms such as "sales," "manager," "profit," "HTML," "marketing," "bilingual," "supply chain," or "call center." With this approach, it'll take only a minute or two for you to determine if this candidate's knowledge, skills, and abilities are in the ballpark or in the fog.

Although there's no question that a candidate who submits masses of information upfront is demonstrating a measure of cluelessness, such candidates can sometimes surprise you. As a result, when candidates send you a virtual suitcase full of information, it's often a sign that they come with a good deal of baggage, but not necessarily. In these instances, it always makes sense to check before you chuck.

Information "Underload"

One of the more bizarre yet surprisingly common tactics used by applicants who appear to be actively pursuing the label of office idiot is to respond to an employment ad with a strong cover letter while omitting a resume. Such candidates are operating under the fallacious assumption that a potential employer will read the cover letter, see that the resume is missing, and then reach out and open a dialogue with the candidate.

Unless a job candidate is actively seeking rejection, this is a ridiculous strategy. In the vast majority of cases, one of the first conclusions that employers reach when candidates only submit a cover letter is that the candidate is careless. The employer typically figures that the applicant responded quickly with a cover letter, forgot to attach anything else, and didn't check his or her work before sending it out. It isn't a major mental leap for the employer to then assume that this type of behavior is typical of this candidate, and since the ad didn't include carelessness as one of the requirements for the position, this candidate is quickly eliminated from consideration.

Other employers will look at this *sans*-resume submission and conclude that the applicant doesn't follow instructions. Employers might also conclude that such a candidate is manipulative, arrogant, lazy, or relatively uninterested in obtaining the job in the first place. Any of these conclusions mean that the candidate is officially out of the running. At the same time, it's possible that the inclusion of an intriguing cover letter, combined with the exclusion of a resume, may induce an employer or two to contact an applicant. The problem is that this is likely to be one or two employers out of a hundred or more. Even in a best-case scenario, all that would happen is that the candidate would be asked to submit a resume. No additional doors would be opened or advantages gained, and the potential opportunities with the 98 or 99 employers who tossed the cover letter aside would be lost forever.

This type of game-playing in the job-search process is best left to the idiotic applicants who are trying to game a potential employer. If you're a job candidate who's thinking about omitting your resume the next time you apply for a job, you're better off omitting that thought.

5

WHO'S THE NEW IDIOT?

New hires can often demonstrate a remarkable facility for engaging in acts of pure office idiocy. However, when dealing with new employees, many current managers, peers, and subordinates are not at a loss when it comes to jumping onto the idiotic bandwagon and demonstrating jerk-like behaviors of their own.

Rumor vs. Reality

For example, let's say your company has just hired a senior manager who has a reputation for being untrustworthy and manipulative. Rumors, hearsay, and legends abound regarding the troubles he caused for his previous employer. Right from the start, you're wondering how this person is going to fit in and, in terms of the bigger picture, why in the world your company even hired him in the first place.

■———————————

Before trying to figure any of this out, the first step is to be sure that the hearsay is accurate. For starters, take a look at the credibility of the sources that have been dispensing this information.

Assuming that the sources check out and the hearsay is true, the next step is to consider the possible reasons why your employer hired this person. For example, perhaps your company rushed the process and simply failed to gather sufficient background data. Or, because this person is supposedly manipulative, perhaps he went into hyper-persuasive mode during the interview. It's also possible that your employer is aware of the hearsay but doesn't believe it. Maybe the person who hired this character believes that any possible problems were due to his previous employer rather than to him, and that he'll thrive in your company. Perhaps this person possesses key skills that your company needs, in spite of the baggage that accompanies them.

Or, is it possible that your company is more underhanded than you thought, and this person will actually fit in perfectly?

To get more of an answer, you should raise your questions about this new hire with your manager. If you're reluctant to do so, that fact alone tells you something about communication and values in your company. If you believe that you have an open and communicative working relationship with your manager, however, you can approach the issue by saying, "I've heard that so-and-so is going to be joining the company. I think there's a lot of interest in knowing more about him and what he's going to be doing here." This is the type of comment that opens a conversation instead of closing it down. It starts with an undeniable fact and then proffers a statement that's actually more of a question. It opens the door for your manager to share her thoughts about this person, as well as the rationale for bringing him onboard.

In the meantime, the reality is that he's joining the company. With that in mind, remember that if you expect to have trouble with him, you'll automatically increase the likelihood of just such an outcome. As a result, once he starts, try to keep your expectations in check and your mind open as you deal with him.

If this new hire turns out to be as bad as his reputation has foretold, his idiotic antics will soon become well-known to everyone. And when that occurs, your current employer is likely to become his former employer.

Instantly Targeted

Another form of rumor that taints the onboarding process comes to life when a departing manager supposedly makes negative comments to a new manager regarding certain current employees. And then, when that new manager is tough on various people, they instantly assume that such treatment is due to whatever their former manager said.

Take the case in which you've got a new manager who leaves you off of e-mails when you should be included, excludes you from meetings that you should attend, and usurps some of your responsibilities without telling you. You do a little probing and hear through the grapevine that your former manager told him some negative things about you.

Before responding, remember that you're more likely to resolve this matter by focusing on the facts than on the fiction that waters most grapevines. While it's possible that your previous manager said derogatory things about you to your new manager, it's also possible that he didn't. There are some valid reasons for meeting with your new manager to discuss this situation, but you shouldn't focus your comments on what your previous manager may or may not have said. Such a discussion is likely to put you in a bad position, literally and figuratively.

Start with a "Q & A" approach by asking questions about various actions that the new manager has taken. With this strategy, you'd say something like, "I'm a little confused over some recent meetings on matters that directly involve my work. I was wondering if I was unintentionally excluded or if there's another plan in place." Notice that this is a nonthreatening and nonaccusatory approach in which you're simply trying to gather information. In making your comments, let your manager see how he can come out ahead by keeping you in the loop, such as by saying, "If I had been at this meeting, I could have prevented the additional costs associated with such-and-such because I had been working on this project all along." To solidify your position, be ready to back up your points with the dates, times, and facts. Notice, also, that this approach isn't whining, complaining, or criticizing; rather, it's problem solving and showing your manager that you can save him time while saving money for the company. And by the way, if you lace your comments with words that are likely to have a positive emotional charge for him, such as "profit," "goals," and "achievement," you're likely to generate an even more favorable reaction.

As a side note, be sure to avoid any comments about your previous manager who may have tried to poison the waters for you. Such comments will only make you look mean, petty, and vindictive, and they would support his negative assertions about you—if he indeed made any.

Going forward, strive for continued excellence in your performance while making sure that your manager is aware of your accomplishments, contributions, and successes.

Badmouthing Behaviors

Moving beyond the realm of rumors and hearsay, there are situations in which new hires engage in idiotic behaviors that do little more than undercut credibility, undermine support, and destroy morale. One of the most common idiotic practices is for new managers to badmouth their predecessors, especially the popular ones. There's absolutely nothing to be gained by such comments, other than disdain and scorn.

Take the case in which a popular manager leaves your company, and you and your fellow employees are all sad to see her go. The company hires a replacement who has a lot to learn about the job, but your biggest complaint is that he keeps saying bad things about your former manager. Although it's evident that most new managers have a good deal to learn about a new job, your new manager has a great deal to learn about managing. Even if the previous manager was terrible, there's nothing to be gained by making disparaging remarks about her.

A new manager is more likely to win the hearts and minds of the team as a result of such factors as his expertise, willingness to listen, ability to understand the employees as individuals, and treating the team fairly and respectfully. Your new manager needs to spend more time on the actions that he'll be taking in his new role, and less time and talk on the actions of the previous manager.

■————————————————————

You don't really need to take action in this case. With each passing day, the new manager will become less and less likely to refer back to the ills and errors of your previous manager. However, this isn't to say that these comments will totally disappear. It's possible that there may be situations years from now when your current manager disparagingly invokes the name of your previous manager when something goes wrong. This is obviously not the hallmark of a great manager, but it still might be heard in the halls of your company.

Nonetheless, if your manager's derogatory comments are seriously grating on you and your coworkers, several of you should meet with him and tell him how you feel. In pursuing this option, the strategy would be to use a businesslike tone, without engaging in a debate over what your previous manager may or may not have done. Rather, you would say something like, "We understand your thoughts about our previous manager; she actually did a lot of good for the department and the company, and we all enjoyed working with her. When you say negative things about her, it kind of grates on us. We really enjoy working with you, and we'd like to focus more on the future than the past."

————————————————————■

This type of wording has three powerful linguistic techniques embedded within it. Firstly, by using the word "and" rather than "but," after the phrase "working with you," the impact of the next phrase is far easier for your manager to internalize and accept. When people hear the word "but" in this context, they're far more likely to react defensively and dismiss whatever follows. Secondly, your concluding sentence has a hidden command, the phrase "focus more on the future than the past." By putting a subtle emphasis on this phrase when you say it, you automatically increase its influence and impact. And finally, by using words that end in "-ly," such as "actually" and "really," you're using terms that are so general that your manager will automatically do his own mental search to fill in the details and assign them meaning that's relevant to him. By doing so, he's likely to be more receptive to the points you're making.

Now Hear This

While new managers are certainly prevalent within the ranks of office idiots, plenty of non-managerial new hires easily meet the criteria required for this dubious distinction. One of the more common forms of this office idiot is the new hire who's constantly complaining to all ears about the company's computers, workspace, policies, procedures, parking, furniture, marketing materials, carpet, or product mix. As luck would *not* have it, one of these office idiots now reports to you.

Even if you are a manager who's more than willing to listen to your employees' complaints, concerns, and suggestions, you are likely to find it difficult to listen to a nonstop barrage of complaints from a newbie. While constant complaining from any employee can be tiring on the ears, inordinate complaints from someone who has not been with the company long enough to find the restroom are particularly galling.

It isn't an automatic problem when new hires voice concerns and offer suggestions. In fact, new hires can often have some sorely needed fresh and creative ideas. The problem occurs when new employees seemingly focus the bulk of their attention on launching an arsenal of complaints, critiques, and ill-founded suggestions. Their comments fall into the annoyance file in short order, and their productivity simply falls by the wayside. Rather than identifying problems, this type of behavior identifies the new employee as the problem.

> To right this ship, your employee needs to understand that you're indeed interested in hearing and reviewing his complaints and concerns, but you're more interested in seeing and reviewing his work. One way to implement a course correction is to ask, "Are you really interested in having your complaints and concerns heard?" He'll most likely say yes. You'd then add, "Good. Do you want to have more credibility and even better suggestions?" And again, his response is likely to be yes. At that point, you'd say, "Great! You're going to be in a much better position to make this happen after you've had more experience in your job and in the company itself. Do you think you can do that?"

By eliciting affirmative responses from this person at various points in the conversation, he's far more likely to say yes at the end. And by wrapping up the discussion with a question that calls for yet another yes while actually proffering a challenge, the employee is practically forced into an affirmative response. And by formally agreeing to make a behavioral change, he's more likely to actually do it.

Major Metamorphosis

Another common phenomenon that occurs with a disproportionate number of new hires is their metamorphosis from excellent job candidate to office idiot. With so many instances of rage across society, it isn't surprising to find that one of the more common metamorphoses is the transition from affable applicant to enraged employee. When employees show rage on the job, most employers today jump on the situation and either get help for the employee or get the employee out of the organization.

The lingering question for employers is how to avoid hiring a potentially explosive office idiot in the future. After all, you can interview an applicant who appears to be personable, calm, professional, and perfect for your open position. During the screening, you're likely to have no idea that such a candidate has issues with anger management. However, once he's on your payroll, you quickly see that he can't manage anything, especially his anger.

One key point to keep in mind is that when candidates are interviewing for jobs, they're in sales mode, and they're saying and doing whatever they can to convince you to hire them. In order to see through some of the superficialities, it's particularly important to make sure that your interview is based on job-related questions that cover an applicant's entire work history. It also helps to not only meet with an applicant a few times, but also to have other employees and members of management interview him or her as well.

When you ask candidates how they handled various challenges in their previous jobs, as well as how they would handle specific problematic situations in the position you're trying to fill, you can occasionally get a glimpse of some underlying tension, not only by what the candidate says, but also by how he or she says it.

You may also be able to uncover glimmers of underlying anger by asking challenging technical questions that are related to the job itself. The way in which the candidate approaches these questions can shed light on some of the darker aspects of his or her personality, especially if he or she responds by degrading your question or your interview style, or if his or her demeanor or facial expression tightens up. The same can be said if you probe some of the less positive aspects of the candidate's work experience, such as the reasons for terminations, possible lack of promotions, or inconsistencies between what is written on the resume and what he says in the interview.

For example, you'd say, "I noticed that your resume says you worked for XYZ Company from 2006 to 2009, but you just said that you left in 2007. Can you please clarify this?" If a person has anger management issues, such an innocuous and appropriate question can be perceived as degrading and accusatory, and hence with the potential to generate an angry response from an individual with a low level of frustration tolerance. When he answers, be on the lookout for nonverbal cues of anger, such as squinty eyes, tightened lips or jaw, or even clenched fists. In looking for tip-offs for suppressed rage, sometimes it's what isn't said that speaks loudest of all.

Nonetheless, there are many individuals who can totally mask their rage, leaving it encapsulated until some trigger sets it off. If none of those triggers are in your screening process, the anger-challenged candidate is likely to skate through.

A totally different strategy that some employers are using to prevent a vast range of problems with new hires is to initially retain them on a temporary basis through an agency. If it seems to be a good match after some period of time, the employee is converted to regular status; if there are issues, the employer simply calls the agency and indicates that this individual's services are no longer needed by the company. This is basically the corporate equivalent of living together before getting married, and it appears to make for a stronger corporate match.

——————————————————————————————————■

Who's in Charge?

Another common player in the gaggle of newly hired office idiots is the new employee who thinks that she's anything but an idiot. This is the new hire who fashions herself as all-knowing, and she's instantly ready to share her purported wisdom with you, while failing to recognize that this isn't a particularly wise step to take.

Take the common case in which a new employee who reports to you is repeatedly telling you how to do your job. In fact, she keeps asking to meet with you to talk further about this very topic. Although you were initially willing to have these types of conversations with her, you're now finding them to be an irritation. At this point, you're looking for the best way to make it stop.

Rather than letting this employee tell you how to do your job, it's time for you to tell her how to do hers. Since her primary responsibilities presumably don't include providing you with counsel and advice, she needs to be informed of this fact. You can do this in a brief discussion with her in which you say, "Look, I appreciate the suggestions. At the same time, we've both got a lot to do, and I can't keep having these conversations. We're really busy, and we need to focus our major attention on doing our own jobs really well. When there's a little time, I'll work out something for us to meet." These comments are team oriented, embedded with recognition and appreciation, and focused on work rather than on her. At the same time, you are advising her that you will be the one who sets up the next get-together. And notice that you have already set the stage for a brief meeting by saying that you'll meet with her "when there's a little time."

Unless you take direct action with her, she's going to continue to bombard you with her pearls of wisdom, most likely at an even more frenetic pace. One piece of wisdom is for you to act more assertively with her. Of course, she's not likely to present that idea to you.

Hi and Bye

It's not as if new employees have the monopoly on acting like office idiots. There are many ways in which current employees can display their own unique brand of idiocy when dealing with new hires. Some of the most common displays of such idiocy are the underhanded behaviors that are designed to push new employees out the door.

For example, let's say that you're a new employee in a company, and you were very happy when you first joined. However, several employees in your department recently approached you and said this is a horrible place to work, especially in terms of the way that management treats people. If you're like most new hires who face these types of comments, you're not sure what to do about them. The initial problem is that instead of having a welcoming committee, employees in your department have established an unwelcoming committee. This is obviously distressing and confusing for any new employee. Although there are many actions that you can take in response to such idiocy, one option that you shouldn't consider is quitting.

In the first place, you don't know if your coworkers are credible. It's possible that their goal is to run off new hires, perhaps to avoid the higher levels of quality or increased output that a new employee may generate. Maybe they have a nasty little clique, and they simply don't want anyone else around. It's important for you to avoid letting their comments tarnish your expectations on this job. If you buy what they're saying and start believing that this is a horrible place to work, you're likely to engage in behaviors that generate a self-fulfilling prophecy.

During this early stage of employment, you should approach the job with an open mind and try to rekindle the enthusiasm, appreciation, and positive attitude that you had when you first joined. After a few months, you'll learn more about the job, your coworkers, and management. You'll be in a better position to know whether the horrible treatment is coming from management or from your coworkers. You'll also be in a much better position to determine your next steps.

Insubordinate Subordinate

In addition to misguided gaggles of office idiots that try to dislodge newly hired employees, there are significant numbers of individual employees who try to generate the same outcome while flying solo. For example, take the case in which you're a new manager in a company, and you're now convinced that one of your employees is trying to make you look bad. Specifically, she made false and degrading statements about the way you handled a particular problem. You also just learned that she was friendly with the manager who held this position before you.

On the one hand, you don't want to start out in this job by firing someone. On the other hand, you definitely want to put an end to this idiotic behavior. Although it's understandable that you don't want to characterize your first days on this job with a termination, you can certainly characterize these days with some disciplinary action when an employee's behavior not only warrants it, but seems to be begging for it.

■————————————————————

This situation calls for an immediate private meeting with her. In such a sit-down session, you should walk through the specifics of her questionable actions and comments, and then let her know the consequences if she continues down this path.

You should wrap up the session with a written warning that spells out her specific acts of insubordination, including dates and witnesses if possible. This warning should include two final sentences with language that reads, "I am very interested in working with you to help correct the issues noted above. However, if you engage in further acts of insubordination, including but not limited to those noted above, there will be more serious disciplinary action, up to and including termination." While this language is harsh and direct, office idiots that engage in this type of behavior with a new manager are not usually swayed by subtlety.

On an administrative note, you and your employee should sign and date this document. Let your employee know that signing it doesn't necessarily mean that she agrees with the contents, but only that the matter has been discussed with her. If she refuses to sign, you should note that on the document and place it in her file.

Importantly, if you take no action and simply let this employee continue to degrade you and your performance, you're essentially allowing and even encouraging this type of behavior, while indicating to everyone else that she is in the right. Otherwise, you'd have taken action to deal with her. In every respect, this employee needs to understand that if she keeps working against you, she won't be working for you.

———————————————————————————————————————■

Closed Door Policy

In addition to job candidates who morph into office idiots after they start working for a company, there are current employees who change from mentors to monsters as soon as the applicant accepts the job offer and reports to work. During the screening process, these managers are friendly, communicative, accessible, and approachable, but they quickly put "un-" in front of each of these adjectives on the employee's first day.

In looking at one of many examples of this type of metamorphosis, take the case in which you're new to a company. Your manager tells you during the interview and again on your first day that you can always come to him if you have questions. He even states that his door is always open. Not surprisingly, you need to speak with him during your first week on the job, so you go to his office but find his door closed. Without giving it a second thought, you knock. (Note that you don't bang on the door as if you were part of the SWAT team; you just give a couple of friendly taps.) When he doesn't answer, you knock again, and that's when the trouble begins. At that instant, he yanks the door open, clearly upset. He tells you that you should never knock on his door when it's closed. This is very different from your old company, and certainly very different from what he told you during the screening process. In spite of what this manager may proclaim during the interview process, the reality is that he doesn't have an actual open door policy; rather, he has an open door policy *except when his door is closed.*

In all fairness, even the most approachable and accessible manager needs to take some time behind closed doors every now and then. This happens during confidential meetings and phone calls, and it's also a strategy that some managers use to manage their time. With that in mind, your manager's desire to avoid interruptions when he has closed his office door isn't necessarily strange or problematic.

However, your manager committed two highly questionable and problematic gaffes in this situation. First, he apparently failed to accurately and fully communicate what he means by his open door policy. All he needed to do was to advise you of this practice, and you'd have refrained from rapping on his door. Unfortunately, many managers flip into office idiot mode when new employees don't telepathically comprehend their unwritten rules. Second, your manager overreacted when you simply knocked on his door. Your action warranted an explanation, and not an explosion. Clearly, his open door policy needs an asterisk to delineate the office idiocy that accompanies it.

In the future, if you need to speak with him and his door is closed, you can send him an e-mail, leave him a voice mail, send him a text message, or simply come back later. And if his door is still closed, you know what to do and, perhaps more importantly, what *not* to do. With any luck, this will end the problem—knock on wood, but not on his door.

6

MEETINGS WITH OFFICE IDIOTS

Meetings are one of the most fertile arenas for office idiots to demonstrate a vast array of behaviors that literally leave most attendees muttering, "We can't go on meeting like this." Office idiots have the finely tuned ability to turn meetings into a mess at every point along the way—before, during, and even long after.

Let's look first at some of the classical idiotic behaviors that go on prior to meetings. During this period, there are widespread opportunities for workplace jerks to disrupt and even derail a meeting before it starts. It's clear that today's office idiots take advantage of every such opportunity.

Jumping the Gun

One of the most popular ways that office idiots create problems with meetings before the flag is up is their tendency to start them ahead of their scheduled time. Take the case in which your manager has an annoying habit of starting meetings five to 10 minutes early. When you show up at the established time, the discussion is already in full force, and your manager gives you a dirty look when you enter. You see yourself as a punctual person, and you're annoyed that your manager starts his meetings early and then looks down on you when you arrive on time. You wonder if it's worth saying something to him about this, or if you should simply let it ride.

On the one hand, there's no question that your manager is entering the realm of office idiocy by scheduling his meetings at one time and then starting them at another. After all, how difficult would it be for him to pick a time and stick to it? It's possible he believes these early starting times will cause employees to be better prepared in his meetings or will lead to shorter meetings. He may also be operating under the assumption that by the time the actual starting time arrives, his meetings are already off to a running start. Of course, the reality is that there's no need to start ahead of time to achieve any of these outcomes.

———————

While this is indeed a case of pre-meeting idiocy, it's also a matter of picking your battles. Do you really want to mix things up with your manager over this idiotic idiosyncrasy? Your manager is apparently wedded to the practice of starting meetings early. As a result, one guaranteed way to end the problem for you is to arrive early. Besides, if the discussions are already going on when you arrive, your fellow employees obviously haven't had any difficulty adjusting to your manager's early liftoffs.

Your manager's tendency to start his meetings five to 10 minutes early is most likely a habit. This means that there really is little that you can say to him that's going to break it. Habits are deeply engrained and enduring, and, as you may have found from attempts to break some of your own habits, an arguably intelligent conversation is unlikely to do much good.

If you still feel compelled to say something to your manager about this, it should be, "I know that you start your meetings five to 10 minutes early, and I'll get there ahead of time going forward." With this approach, your manager can only agree with what you're saying, and you'll have defused any possible negativity that may have been brewing as a result of your "late" arrivals. And if by some miracle he isn't aware of the fact that he's starting these meetings ahead of schedule, you've updated him without humiliating him.

In every respect, if you don't want any more dirty looks from your manager, you can solve the problem in five or 10 minutes.

See You Later

Along with the legions of office idiots who start their meetings early, there's an equally compelling batch of idiotic attendees whose credo compels them to show up late, sometimes very late, for every meeting.

Let's assume for a minute that you're a manager who holds regular meetings with your fellow managers. You repeatedly find that several of your associates have no qualms about arriving late. You've spoken to them about this, and you've tried all sorts of persuasive strategies to get them to change their ways—and their watches. By this time, they know that you regard their tardiness as rude, callous, inconsiderate, disruptive, and downright nasty. But they also know that they're still going to be late to your next meeting.

Before looking at these attendees, the first step is to take a hard look at your meetings. This is a perfect time to revisit their content, length, format, timing, and objectives, along with the need for each invited individual to actually attend. One of the most important questions about any meeting is whether it needs to be held at all. If your meetings focus on updates and reviews, they could probably be replaced with memos, phone calls, or e-mail. Meetings tend to be more effective for topics that require joint decision-making or problem-solving.

If you take the kind-hearted approach and delay the start of your meetings until the stragglers arrive, you're simply rewarding the tardy bunch and punishing those who show up on time. This will cause more and more managers to show up late—not a good strategy, obviously. The key is to let all of the invitees know when your meetings will start and end, and then stick to that schedule no matter what. Send out a reminder before each meeting, along with the agenda. At the meeting, keep the discussion moving, on track, and on time.

If various attendees still arrive late, don't stop the meeting to provide them with a recap. Rather, tell the late arrivals, "Let's meet later, and I'll fill you in on what you missed," and then go right back to where you were when the late arrivals decided to grace everyone with their presence.

Besides, if you give a late arrival a recap, are you going to provide another recap when the next office idiot arrives 10 minutes after that? And what about the idiots that follow?

Bottom Drawer Treatment

Not only is it a good idea to send an agenda to the attendees prior to a meeting, but in many cases it's also worthwhile to ask the attendees for their input regarding the topics to be discussed. However, even in cases where managers take both of these steps, there's still a major opportunity for office idiocy.

One of the most common examples occurs with weekly meetings. Let's say that your manager holds weekly departmental meetings and asks you and your associates for topics to be placed on the agenda. You e-mail some suggested topics to him, and that's where the trouble starts. The bottom line is that your manager always places your topics at the bottom of the agenda. As a result, by the time your topics are finally reached, the meeting is practically over and everyone is ready to go. At that point, your manager asks you to give a quick summary. You rush through your comments, glossing over points that warrant discussion, and then throw the topics open for comments. Since your manager has made it clear that your topics are not particularly important, and since everyone is ready to go, it's assumed that your cursory overview of the topics will suffice. Perhaps he asks if there are any comments, and everyone looks around and says nothing. Then, it's game over. Everyone gets up and exits, leaving you and your items in the dust.

On the one hand, your manager is taking the right step by soliciting input from attendees upfront regarding the issues to be discussed in a forthcoming meeting. And it's definitely a good idea for you to submit topics that merit inclusion on the agenda. The problem is that your manager is running these meetings like a classic office idiot. He doesn't allocate sufficient time to cover all of the topics, and he apparently has little sense of priorities when finalizing the agenda.

It appears that your manager needs more information on the topics that you suggest. He doesn't understand the significance of the issues that you'd like to include, and that makes it much easier for him to drop them to the bottom of the agenda and then ignore them when their time for discussion arrives.

One strategy is for you to do more than submit topics to your manager. When he asks for suggestions regarding the subjects to be discussed in these meetings, you should submit your topics plus a brief sentence or bullet point that highlights their importance, impact, and degree of urgency. Another strategy is to simply act more assertively during these meetings. By going along with your manager's request and quickly summarizing your agenda items, you're setting the stage for you and your topics to be dismissed. Rather than rushing through your points while most of the attendees are packing to leave, you should say what's really on your mind, such as, "We've got some important issues that still need to be addressed. Are all of you able to stay a little longer to discuss them, or would you prefer to have a separate meeting during the week?"

Notice that this is a forced-choice question. With this phrasing, it isn't a matter of whether to meet to discuss your topics; it's simply a matter of when. Will it be now or later?

Pulling the Rug Out

There are also office idiots who organize meetings and set up specific times for key participants to make a presentation, only to totally change the ground rules and expectations at the last minute.

Take the case in which your manager has scheduled some off-site meetings to build communication, coordination, and cooperation across department lines. As part of this program, he asks you to put together a one-hour presentation for the group. After spending many hours on this project, the day of the meeting arrives and you're good to go. However, five minutes before show time, your manager tells you that time is running short and you need to make your presentation very brief—no more than 20 minutes. As a result, you rush through the whole thing, and it doesn't go well.

This ends up being embarrassing for you, and you feel that this flop was your manager's fault. And to make matters worse, he makes a passing comment to you indicating that it's unfortunate that your presentation didn't go so well. You bite your tongue at the time, but you'd like to tell him that he's to blame for your poor showing.

■————————————————

As tempting as it would be to place blame squarely on your manager, such an exercise is always destined to be futile. The act of blaming others typically makes the blamer look like the idiot, even if he or she had absolutely nothing to do with a negative outcome. Besides, if you point the finger of blame at your manager, he's likely to claim that your presentation was the problem, and that you need to be flexible enough to handle last-minute changes. From that point, the blaming turns into verbal ping pong, and nothing is accomplished or resolved, other than your manager becoming even more upset with you.

Rather than focusing on blame, you'll find more satisfaction and success by focusing on steps you can take right now to deal with the problems that resulted from the change of plans. For example, if you rushed through your slides, charts, or tables, one step is to forward a copy to all of the attendees, perhaps with some annotations to clarify your findings, analyses, and recommendations. As part of this follow-up, you should invite these attendees to contact you if they have questions or need further information.

At the same time, be sure to look down the road and think about how you'll deal with this type of situation in the future. For example, if your manager is known for making last-minute changes, you'll need to stay in touch with him as you prepare future presentations, all the while emphasizing the importance of having your full timeslot. And as you work on your presentation, ask yourself one key question: *What will I do if my manager cuts my time in half?*

———————————————————————————————■

The Clueless Know-It-All

One of the more common species of office idiots that inhabit meetings is the blowhard who tries to present an aura of being the all-knowing personification of wisdom. What this person doesn't realize, of course, is that truly wise people don't have to flash their brilliance to others; it simply shines. People who constantly try to show the world how smart they are actually do little more than show how insecure they are. Although they're trying to convince those around them that they're beacons of knowledge, they're actually just trying (unsuccessfully) to convince themselves.

Let's say you go to a department meeting and instantly feel a churning in the pit of your stomach when your all-knowing coworker enters and sits down. This person has established a tradition of disrupting every meeting he attends, fashioning himself as a big thinker who doesn't need to listen to anyone. He incessantly spews out ideas that are off the wall and off the mark, often just for the sake of argument, and in spite of the fact that he's totally wrong.

When you encounter a know-it-all in a meeting, and he's pontificating ad nauseam, the first question that comes to mind is clear: Where is the leader in all of this? While open and robust meetings are a lofty goal, if one attendee's mouth is the main thing that's open in these meetings, that's a problem. And when a participant is disrupting, disturbing, and derailing a meeting, it's time for the leader to show some leadership.

After all, there's a descriptor for your coworker's idiotic behaviors, in which he incessantly pushes his opinion on others, refuses to listen, and ignores the fact that he's ruining the meeting. Such antics are called *self-oriented behaviors*. Rather than focusing on meeting the needs of the meeting, self-oriented behaviors are focused on meeting the needs of the person who engages in them. Employees who demonstrate this type of behavior can be counted on for one thing: repeat performances.

Rather than waiting for the next showing, you and some of your fellow employees should have a separate meeting with your manager to express your concern, backed up with examples of the behaviors, dates when they occurred, and their impact on the group's performance. Your manager needs to see the negative impact and costs associated with your colleague's know-it-all actions, as well as the benefits associated with reining him in. Such benefits include more focused meetings, more creative thinking and decision-making, increasingly productive meetings, and better overall use of the time.

With this foundation in place, you should use a Socratic approach by asking your manager, "Is there anything that all of us can do to help deal with this situation?" This type of question automatically assumes the existence of a problem while focusing the discussion on the steps you and your colleagues can take in order to help solve it. As you discuss options with your manager, be sure to let him know that you'll support him if he opts to take more direct action to deal with this individual. By sensing that he has your support, he'll be more likely to step things up a notch.

As a side note, it's important to remember that some disagreement in a meeting can be healthy and productive. A little conflict can avoid groupthink, a phenomenon in which everyone blithely agrees with whatever is said, leading to minimal thinking, marginal creativity, and modest results. A little disagreement helps propel a meeting along a far more creative and productive path, forcing attendees to come up with new and different ways to solve problems. However, this is a far cry from the disagreement that emanates from the interminable ranting of a know-it-all. In such meetings, "groupthink" has an entirely different meaning. Namely, what does the group think about the know-it-all? They think he's an idiot.

Targeted for Taunts

Another common pest that thrives in many meetings is the predator. This is the office idiot who uses meetings as a launching pad for insults, taunts, and degrading comments. Such jerks have no qualms about targeting fellow employees for an unwarranted and totally inappropriate volley of verbal venom.

Let's say you're attending a meeting and another attendee starts taking pot-shots at you. His comments may deal with work that you completed, work that you didn't complete, or work that was never even assigned to you in the first place, as well as an array of personal taunts targeting your work habits or hours.

■————————————————————

When you're subjected to this type of office idiocy during a meeting, the first question actually focuses on another idiot—namely, the person who's running the show. It's his or her responsibility to put an immediate stop to this nonsense. Because you're dealing with two office idiots, there are two strategies to apply. One is to ignore the outrageous assault and simply turn to whoever is running the meeting and shrug your shoulders and raise your eyebrows imploringly. This form of nonverbal communication says that you're not going to lower yourself to the level of the attacker and respond to his ridiculous comments. The second strategy involves indicating to whoever is running the meeting that it's time for him or her to deal with this idiot.

If you ignore the office idiot's bellicose comments, you're depriving him of the satisfaction associated with insulting you and getting you upset. In essence, you're preventing him from gratifying his need to dominate and control. As a result, since his behavior isn't meeting his needs, he's actually less likely to keep engaging in it.

At the same time, you may find it difficult to sit still in the face of a verbal attack and say nothing, especially if the individual who's running the meeting is somehow allowing the attacker to run off his mouth. This leads to the second approach, in which you respond to this attacker on the spot but without becoming defensive or upset. Once again, if you demonstrate either of the latter reactions, the attacker is going to sense that he's getting to you, and this will only encourage him to continue or even magnify the assault.

A more effective approach is to calmly respond to his comments, but do so with questions. After he drops one of his verbal bombs on you, ask him specific questions about such assertions, especially with open-ended questions that start with when, where, how, and why. When his responses stray from the truth, you should spring the reality trap by saying something like this: "Interesting, but here's what actually happened. Do you want to see the e-mail that I sent right after this?"

The more you deal in facts, dates, and evidence, the more foolish this office idiot is going to look. Since looking like a jerk isn't particularly satisfying to him, and since that's going to be the outcome whenever he strikes out at you in these meetings, again, he is going to have less incentive to do so.

Being a Bobblehead

Another category of managers who easily qualify as charter members of the society of office idiots share a particularly absurd tactic when running meetings. They talk from start to finish, rarely pausing for any input or inquiry from the attendees. They pontificate the entire time, expecting the employees to sit quietly, filled with awe. Indeed, rather than finding such meetings to be awe-filled, employees simply find them to be awful.

Let's take a situation in which your manager holds meetings where her voice is the only one that's heard. It's easy to regard these meetings as a waste of time, since they're devoid of the interaction that's required for productive group analyses and problem-solving. After all, when meetings are nothing more than a matter of listening to your manager's sermons, e-mail would certainly suffice.

■——————————————————

Because you're not going to change your manager's behavior during one of these sessions, you and some of your coworkers should have a separate meeting with her to discuss your concerns and suggestions. At that time, you'd say something like, "We think your ideas are great. When you're talking, it gets us thinking about applying what you are saying, and this gets us to come up with new solutions that make your comments even more powerful. Is there a way for us to do more dialoguing with you during your meetings?"

This wording has several compelling components to help sway her thinking. You open with a respectful comment that will elicit a nod from her, followed by noting your interest in building on what she is saying. This is likely to be inherently palatable to her (notice that it's a far cry from whining that you never get a chance to talk during her meetings). You also include the word "powerful," which has a highly positive emotional charge for most people in management. And finally, you wrap up your comments with a low-key question, rather than with an answer. Also, your question includes the word "dialoguing," a term that is far more collaborative than just asking if you can do more of the talking during her meetings.

And as noted previously, another strategy that helps introduce lasting behavioral changes is introducing them on a trial basis. With this in mind, you and your associates should ask your manager if she'd be willing to experiment with more dialoguing in her meetings for the next couple of weeks. Tell her if she doesn't see markedly improved results by that time, you'd be glad to return to the current format. This is a tempting offer, and because the risk to her is so low, she's likely to give it a shot. And when she does, you and your coworkers should be ready to fully immerse yourselves in these meetings and do all in your power to come up with some stellar ideas.

What Did You Say?

Not only do office idiots showcase their idiocy during meetings; they often bring it to center stage after a meeting has ended and its contents are little more than an echo. For example, take the situation in which you attend a departmental meeting, find the discussion to be interesting and productive, but don't make any comments at the time. This shouldn't be a problem for anyone, other than an office idiot.

Speaking of idiots, your manager comes up to you after the meeting and sarcastically thanks you for your important contributions. Apparently, he wants employees to speak up in his meetings, even if they're spewing inane or ridiculous comments, rather than sitting, listening intently, and absorbing whatever is being discussed.

Although it's ridiculous for your manager to toss this kind of insult at anyone after a meeting, it's helpful to look at it in the context of his overall style. He may regard his comment as a friendly and humorous throwaway that he makes to everyone, especially those whom he likes and can "take it." In fact, in some cases, managers are more likely to toss playful comments at employees who are doing well as opposed to those who are doing poorly. If this sounds like his style—even though, granted, his comment is a little goofy—you should ignore it.

However, it's also important to examine the tone of his comment. If his words truly sound negative and insulting, rather than playfully sarcastic, and if he tends to direct this type of unwanted verbiage toward you and not your fellow employees, then it's time to take a look at your overall working relationship with him and see if some repairs are in order. For example, if there are issues regarding your performance and productivity, he may be transferring his negativity in those areas into sarcasm.

Or, perhaps he's a manager who expects or even demands active participation in his meetings, and, for better or worse, he has issues when employees don't jump into the discussion. If this sounds like him, you may want to run a mental replay of the meeting to see if you missed any opportunities where your input may have been warranted, and then keep that in mind for the next meeting.

If his specious thank-you is gnawing away at you, you also have the option of talking to him about it. However, if you do, it shouldn't be in the framework of a formally scheduled meeting to discuss this single comment. Rather, as you're talking with him about other work-related matters, you can say something like, "Hey, by the way, I really thought your meeting had all sorts of good info, but I was more absorbed in listening and learning than throwing in a comment that probably would not have advanced the discussion. I just don't want you to think that I was zoning out." This type of comment, with its embedded compliment, will help set the record straight for your manager while giving you some closure, as well.

Besides, everyone who attends a meeting prefers attendees who say nothing over those who jump in just to hear themselves talk. The same applies to idiotic leaders of meetings and their inane and insulting comments after a meeting has ended.

Replaying Your Mistakes

It's not only the leaders of meetings who engage in post-meeting idiocy. There can be any number of office idiots who attend these meetings and then go on to ply their idiocy long after adjournment. One of the more prevalent forms of such idiocy is the prolonged teasing, taunting, and harassment of anyone who makes the slightest mistake, errant comment, or casual slip-up during the meeting.

For example, let's say you make a presentation at a meeting that is attended by several of your coworkers. As you work your way through the slides, it becomes evident to everyone that you made a mistake in one of your calculations. It's a careless and minor goof, and it doesn't influence the major points or conclusions of your presentation, but it's a mistake nonetheless.

Fast-forward two weeks, and you find that you're still being teased about this miniscule error, and you're not delighted. In response, you basically tell your cohorts that this whole incident is old news and it's time to let it go, but the idiots and their idiocy continue. This type of teasing can cover a broad spectrum that ranges from playful banter to serious insults. However, the nature of the teasing isn't as important as its impact; if you find that it's hurtful, embarrassing, upsetting, and even keeping you up at night, then it's time to take more specific action to deal with it.

Becoming upset with verbal abuse, however "humorous" it's intended to be, isn't altogether surprising in light of recent research findings that indicate that the emotional pain associated with verbal assaults registers in the same part of the brain that processes physical pain. In essence, sticks and stones can break your bones, and names can hurt you, too.

It's particularly revealing to look at whatever may be motivating office jerks to seize the opportunity to give you verbal grief in the first place. For the most part, these individuals are insecure, jealous, and seeking a way to convince themselves that they have some power and significance. In addition, by focusing their attention on teasing you, they're able to divert attention away from their own deficiencies, shortcomings, and failures.

One of the best ways to deal with this kind of idiocy is to ignore it. The reality is that your coworkers are going to continue the harangues if they sense that their comments are making you upset. That's the exact reaction and reward that they seek, and as long as they get it from you, they're likely to continue. If you can ignore the comments, shrug them off, or give no reaction at all, you'll be taking away that reward, and that's likely to extinguish the teasing. Besides, soon enough, someone else is going to make a slipup in front of them, and then these taunting office idiots will focus their unwanted and misdirected attention on them.

However, if you feel that you simply can't let it go, especially if the teasing has continued for several weeks, you can take a more direct approach. The next time this old news is dredged up and dumped on you, just respond by saying, "You must be getting tired of this, aren't you?" This is actually a very powerful question. First, it's noncombative but contains an embedded command that tells the idiots that they must be coming to the end of this activity. Second, the rhetorical nature of the question literally forces the idiots to say yes; after all, if they say no, it's a clear admission of stupidity and pettiness. While such characteristics are indeed trademarks of office idiots, they don't typically make public proclamations to this effect.

7

OFFICE IDIOTS AND THEIR E-MAIL

The world of e-mail offers idiots an endless landscape in which they not only display their idiocy, but do so through a medium that allows their foolishness to endure forever. Rather than simply saying something incredibly ridiculous, inane, insulting, or profane that gradually falls into the realm of hearsay, e-mail creates a documented trail of idiocy that will endure for generations.

When you ask people what the "e" in e-mail stands for, they'll typically give you a patronizing smirk and smugly reply, "Electronic." Wrong! Perhaps that's the technical definition, but in reality, the "e" in e-mail stands for "evidence." If you're ever looking for proof of office idiocy, you'll find plenty of it in e-mail messages. So will a jury.

For All the World to See

One of the more flagrant displays of office idiocy via e-mail is the virtual version of public humiliation. This is accomplished by office idiots who send harsh and critical e-mail messages to their employees and simultaneously copy hordes of onlookers.

For example, let's assume that your manager sends you an e-mail that rips into your work on a recent project. As an added kicker, he copies most of your fellow employees. In light of this jerkiness, it would not be surprising to find that you're more than a little upset and embarrassed. And besides, you don't even think your work on the project was so bad.

Your manager actually made two mistakes in this situation. First, although e-mail is often excellent for conveying facts, figures, and data, it falls far short as a vehicle to convey criticism, disagreements, arguments, or emotions. If a manager wants to provide negative feedback to an employee, the interaction will be far more productive when handled face-to-face. The second mistake was copying your coworkers on this rant. It's totally inappropriate to reprimand employees in front of others, whether in person or online. Public humiliation generates little more than anger, dissatisfaction, and embarrassment, and these reactions don't do much for building motivation, productivity, performance, or loyalty.

There's no question that you should discuss your concerns with your manager, provided that you do so in a businesslike and constructive manner. Rather than simply saying how upset and hurt you feel, you should first give your manager the facts about your performance on the project in question. If your manager has drawn some false conclusions about your work, you should correct them.

As for the negative e-mail, there's nothing wrong with telling your manager that negative feedback is best presented and received in private and in person. You can tell him that face-to-face feedback has several advantages, especially since there's a far greater chance that feedback will be fully understood, time will be saved, resistance and resentment will be greatly reduced, and the likelihood of similar problems will be diminished, if not eliminated.

If he somehow disagrees—and that's a real possibility since he has already demonstrated that he's an office idiot—you should say, "I'm curious. If your manager sent you an e-mail that blasted your work and he included most of your coworkers, what would you say?" Then stop talking. His answer is going to tell you exactly what you should then say to him. It's also going to tell you a great deal about him.

Let Your E-mail Do the Talking

Another particularly annoying display of office idiocy is the person who rarely reads incoming e-mail, loses it half the time, and then keeps asking for the same information over and over again.

Take the situation in which one of your fellow employees repeatedly requests information that you previously e-mailed to him several times. Now that another request from this person has arrived in your mailbox, you're wondering if you should simply start a new e-mail and include the information, or if you should go back to your original e-mail and forward it again. You decide that you want your colleague to see that you already sent the information to him, so you forward your original e-mail. After all, by doing so, you're saving time for yourself while providing him with a gentle reminder that he received this information from you in the past. That should be the end of the issue, but when office idiots receive forwarded e-mail in this context, they instantly think it's rude. As a result, your colleague runs to your manager and plays the rudeness card in describing what you just did. Now what?

Before firing off any e-mail or comments that you may come to regret, step back and consider one important fact about the recipient: rather than admitting that he has not been diligent in handling the information that you've been sending to him, he's trying to deflect any negative attention that might come his way by claiming that you're rude. Unless you included some nasty remarks in the body of the message you sent, he's the one who's rude. After all, if anyone did anything wrong here, it's your coworker who can't keep track of what you've sent him. And if anyone's manager needs to be contacted about questionable behavior, it's his.

If the situation degenerates to the point that your manager wants to discuss it with you, be sure to bring copies of the e-mail in question. In this case, just let your e-mail do the talking. Your manager should have no problem determining where the problem literally and figuratively lies.

E-mail Battles

Another common manifestation of idiocy in this arena is the tendency for workplace jerks to engage in prolonged wars of words via e-mail. These are often no-win encounters, and this means that those who heed the calls to these battles are typically the losers.

For example, let's say your manager and coworkers get into heated e-mail arguments, and they keep trying to drag you into them. These virtual fisti-cuffs go back and forth, and you typically have to scroll far down to find out how a particular flare-up even started in the first place.

In reality, the best way to handle an e-mail battle is to stay out of it. After all, try to think of an e-mail conflict in which one party finally e-mailed the other and admitted, "Come to think of it, you're right." It doesn't turn out that way. E-mail battles exacerbate issues and make them more intense and inflamed. As noted previously, although e-mail is great for facts, figures, strategies, plans, or documentation, it's typically the worst medium for emotions, disagreements, or arguments. Far too many of the components required for effective communication are missing from the medium. E-mail is but one channel of communication, and effective communication often calls for more. Further, by relying only on printed words, many of the critical elements of feedback are missing, and that's enough to undercut any effort at real communication. After all, a great deal of communication is based on nonverbal factors, such as body language, tone, volume, and cadence, all of which are sorely lacking in e-mail.

As a result, when you see the virtual winds of war blowing in an e-mail message, you should either pick up your phone or pick up your feet and deal directly with the combatants.

As a side note, when a manager engages in e-mail jousting, the underlying message to everyone else is that e-mail is an acceptable arena in which battles can be waged.

E-Expletives

One of the more distressing components of e-mail battles is the tendency of some office idiots to lace their comments with profanity. Whether it's out of rage, immaturity, or pure cluelessness, these jerks load their e-mail with venomous and scurrilous language that has no place in the workplace—or anywhere else.

Let's say that you just received an e-mail from your manager, and he's upset with the way you handled one of your projects. You think you did a fairly good job, but his e-mail is hostile and laced with profanity from start to finish. Right from the top, even if you did less than a "fairly good" job on your project, there's nothing good about a manager who responds with e-mail that's replete with profanities. Sooner or later, this type of outburst is going to come back and bite him and probably bite the company as well. In fact, such a message can form the basis of a bullying claim, and instead of swearing, your manager is likely to be swearing-in. Besides, if your manager isn't satisfied with your performance, he shouldn't be giving you feedback by e-mail in the first place. Rather, he should either meet with you one-on-one or at least speak with you by phone. And the focus should be on performance, behaviors, and results.

With all of this in mind, you should have a sit-down meeting with your manager to discuss the performance in question, as well as the ways to further strengthen future performance. Such a meeting will also provide you with an opportunity to voice your concerns about his propensity toward profanity.

Rather than sugarcoating your comments or meekly stating that you don't like profanity, the idea is to use a firm and businesslike approach. It can be as direct as saying, "I do have to say that I think profanity in e-mail is offensive and upsetting, and not just to me." Once you make this statement, your next move is not to move. Rather, stop talking and don't say anything at all until he replies. Your silence at this point will say far more than any words that come to mind.

Importantly, your statement is specifically designed to avoid inflaming a potentially explosive situation. As well, it doesn't include the word "you." When people are being given this type of feedback and hear the word "you," they're far more likely to react defensively. Instead of using "you," this approach replaces it with "I." You're still getting the message across loud and clear, while the barriers and blockages associated with the often accusatory use of the word "you" are all removed.

As a side note, there is a reason why this should be a sit-down meeting. When people are sitting down, they're less likely to become incensed, explosive, and hostile. That said, if your manager just sits there or responds with anything other than an apology, you should unequivocally state you don't want any more e-mail that's laden with profanity. And if he continues to resort to cursing and clicking Send, you should resort to meeting with his manager or the HR manager.

Indecipherable Messages

Another way that office idiots create problems through e-mail comes from their inability or refusal to write clearly and correctly. Interestingly, jerks whose e-mail is filled with grammatical, spelling, and syntactical errors often react negatively when given feedback on this matter. They apparently operate under the absurd assumption that people who can't decipher their muddled messages are actually launching a personal attack.

For example, take the case in which e-mail messages from your manager are filled with spelling and punctuation errors, and his word choices are often vague and unclear. However, if you respond by e-mail and ask for clarification, he ignores you. And if you call him or go see him, he treats you poorly and acts as if you're the problem.

■————————————————————

Because it isn't uncommon to find that office idiots literally and figuratively close the door to employee overtures on this matter, the easiest and most productive step is for you to simply work with the e-mail that he writes. After all, it would be difficult enough to improve his ability to craft cogent e-mails if he were interested and motivated to do so. The fact that he's this resistant means that his garbled e-mail messages are here to stay. If you're here to stay, you need to cope with them.

With that in mind, you should regularly e-mail your manager and let him know the steps you're taking as a result of his e-mail, and then cite his exact language as well as the date of the message. With this approach, you'll be better able to align your work with his expectations. Further, by working with this office idiot's incoherent and inept e-mail, you'll actually find that you're building your skills in understanding what he's saying, in much the same way that a parent can understand their children's early attempts at language, while others have no idea what they're saying.

In addition, by communicating clearly and effectively with your manager regarding his muddled messages, your comments/feedback just might strengthen his writing skills in some small way. Of course, the final advantage of more frequent e-mail communiqués with him is the protection such messages will afford if the outcome of your action is not to his liking.

From BCC to CC

One consistent source of e-mail crises, conflicts, and chaos is centered on the use of the dreaded BCC. Although it seems simple enough to purposely include a fellow employee under the radar in an e-mail exchange, in most cases it's just a matter of time before that person flies onto the radar screen, at which point everything flies out of hand.

For example, let's say you're e-mailing back and forth with a coworker regarding a departmental problem, and he's being stubborn and illogical. When you get tired of bashing your head against this virtual wall, you decide that you want one of your associates to see this idiocy—not to have her participate, but just to give her an FYI. Unfortunately, rather than viewing your e-mail as an FYI, your coworker views it as an invitation. So, she jumps right in and e-mails her thoughts to you and the other coworker. She takes the "B" out of "BCC," and you take a serious hit.

As a rule, when an employee receives a BCC, he or she shouldn't enter the discussion. Period. However, there are plenty of office idiots who operate under the gross misconception that as long as they're copied on an e-mail, their input is sought.

Looking at this situation from the standpoint of prevention, the best way to avoid a repeat performance is to ask yourself one question whenever you're thinking about BCCing one of your associates:

What will happen if she jumps into the conversation? If you shudder over such a possibility, no matter how remote, stay away from the BCC. If you still feel compelled to use this feature down the road, it's essential to use it very discretely. Always remember that a lapse in judgment, a cursory reading, or a simple mistake by an office idiot can create a huge problem in an instant.

By the way, in the current situation, you'd need to follow up with two people. First, you should meet with the individual who received your BCC and jumped into the dialogue. Let her know that this was a confidential e-mail to her, and her failure to treat it as a BCC created additional problems in an already problematic situation. (And, of course, don't ever BCC her again!) You should also meet with your allegedly stubborn and illogical coworker and apologize for the BCC. You may also want to use this opportunity to continue the discussion in which he was showing such obstinacy. After all, the discussion sounded like it really belonged in a face-to-face setting in the first place.

———————————————————————————■

Tone It Down

Another type of e-mail idiocy that's wildly successful in generating negativity has to do with its tone. While the actual words might not be antagonistic, arrogant, or dismissive, the subtext and tone can cause the recipient to perceive it as being mean, distasteful, or nasty. If you receive this type of an e-mail, one of the quickest and easiest conclusions is that the sender is an office idiot.

In many cases, this is the truth.

For example, take the case in which you receive e-mails from a high-ranking person in your company that come across with a snarky tone. You'd be fully justified in thinking that the sender is trying, however subtly, to put you down or make you feel inferior.

On the one hand, there are indeed office idiots who hide behind the safety of a keyboard to launch all sorts of subtly (and not-so-subtly) insulting, degrading, or condescending messages. The best way to deal with these office idiots is to avoid responding in kind online, as that only intensifies the problem. (Refer to the previous discussion on e-mail wars on page 100.) A better step is to either call or visit the sender and discuss the matter. In such a discussion, you'd open the conversation by bringing a copy of the e-mail with you and saying, "I'm a little confused over this e-mail, and I wanted to make sure there's not a problem. And if there is one, I want to correct it." Once again, this non-threatening approach features plenty of "I's" and no "you's." It'll open the door to a discussion of whether there's an issue, and if so, what it is and how it can be corrected. By avoiding a personal attack and taking a businesslike, constructive, and fact-based approach, your messages will be so non-threatening that even an office idiot is likely to buy into them.

At the same time, there are situations in which an e-mail message can appear to be mean, when, in reality, it isn't. If you receive an e-mail from an associate whose messages always seem to have a mean tone, you're likely to feel yourself clench up before you even open it. After all, you already believe that the content and tone will be negative. Although it's entirely possible that the message has a negative tone, it's also possible that your expectations are tainting what you read. The problem is that if you expect an e-mail message to have a negative tone, you instantly increase the likelihood of finding it. For example, even a sentence as innocuous as "You did a good job" can easily be perceived negatively if that's what you expect from the sender.

As a first course of action in this type of situation, try to avoid instantly assuming that e-mail from this individual is going to be negative. If you feel yourself tightening up at the sight of e-mail from this individual, take a deep breath, relax your shoulders, and try to read the e-mail as slowly and in as positive a tone as possible. You may be surprised by what you see, hear, and feel.

Who's on First?

Then there's the totally petty side of e-mailing. Leading the pettiness parade are the office idiots who complain about the ordering of the names in messages sent to multiple recipients.

Here's a typical example: You send an e-mail to your manager and several other non-management employees, and your manager gets upset because his name was not listed first. And just to be sure there's no doubt about his idiocy and insecurity, he seals the deal by contacting you for the sole purpose of saying that because he's the senior individual among the recipients, his name should be number one. By informing you of the importance of placing his name first on such e-mail, he's unwittingly telling you that he has some underlying issues in terms of self-confidence, self-esteem, and personal security. If he were truly comfortable in his skin as a manager, he would not have even noticed where his name was on your e-mail.

Unfortunately, there are many managers out there who line up with your manager on this one. In fact, some of these managers believe that if their name appears after the name of a lower-level employee, the sender is using a passive-aggressive strategy to send them a degrading message. Although the message you're trying to send is in the body of the text rather than in the listing of addressees, your manager apparently sees things differently.

Interestingly, it's also possible that the culture of your company reinforces this sentiment by having an unwritten expectation that employees' names in e-mail should be listed in rank order. Some may even contend that doing so is part of e-mail etiquette. However, even if this is the case, who'd make a big deal about it? The cadres of office idiots who are in a little over their heads, apparently.

With that in mind, whether your company has an unwritten rule about this or not, you're still dealing with a situation in which your manager expects to be in the lead position when he's the most senior recipient of an e-mail. Although it's a clear display of office idiocy for any manager to have a hissy fit over a matter that's so remarkably insignificant, he's still your manager. Since this simple matter is so simple to resolve, the best step is to place him in the first spot. By doing so, you'll avoid placing yourself in a more difficult spot.

TMI (Too Much Information)

Then there are office idiots whose e-mail messages go on and on forever. When it comes to crafting such messages, these jerks have no filters at all. If it's on their mind, it's on their monitor—and yours. They waste all sorts of time crafting their endless messages, followed by more time wasted by the recipients who try to figure out what in the world they're saying.

For example, you open an e-mail from one of your brevity-challenged employees, and your monitor instantly fills up with her words. You're curious as to where this virtual diatribe ends, so you scroll down...and down...and down. One immediate question is why some employees feel compelled to put every conceivable thought in their e-mails. It turns out that there are a number of possible explanations. In some cases, these are highly dependent individuals who have a fear of making a mistake. They believe that if they say as much as possible in an e-mail, they'll cover whatever the issue may be without leaving anything out. The fact that they fill their e-mail with unimportant information, as well as the fact that doing so is actually a mistake, totally escapes them.

This excessive virtual verbosity can also sometimes be caused by sheer laziness. After all, it takes more thought, effort, and time to write a clear and concise message than it does to throw everything into an e-mail and let the receiver figure out what's important.

As a manager of one of these office idiots, it's appropriate for you to advise her to do some editing before hitting Send, but you're likely to find that advising her to cut down her e-mails is not going to cut it. The problem is that if she lacks the skills to do so, all you're doing is repeating yourself. And that reminds her of how she writes.

Rather than focusing on telling her what to do, a more productive strategy is to show her how. For example, just for starters, give her three simple tips for writing shorter and more effective e-mail by 1) spelling out the objective of her message before writing anything, 2) using bullet points, and 3) reading her e-mail aloud prior to sending it. It's also helpful to provide her with specific feedback on the e-mail she sends you, and even show her some editorial changes that will help streamline her messages. If you're fortunate enough to see some improvement in her e-mail, be sure to provide her with positive feedback. This will further encourage her to keep her e-mail on target rather than on everything else.

8

IDIOTIC MANAGERIAL PRACTICES

Whether their training comes from academic programs, seminars, previous bosses, television shows, or fortune cookies, there are armies of idiotic managers whose skills, expertise, and managerial practices are so primitive that even a Neanderthal would shake his head and wonder how he came in second behind such creatures. These managers often mask their idiocy by packaging their actions in *au courant* managerial parlance, but their performance is still something out of the Precambrian past.

The Dumping Ground

One of the more common players in this cast of clowns is the manager who picks up on a little factoid concerning the way in which additional responsibilities can help employees learn and grow. And then, securely embracing his dearth of knowledge, he reaches a totally specious conclusion: the more responsibilities that are heaped onto an employee, the more he or she will grow.

For example, take the case in which a fellow employee quits, and your manager seizes on this departure as golden opportunity to flash his managerial magnificence by dumping virtually all of this former employee's responsibilities onto you. "This will be a stretch for you," he says, "but it's an opportunity to grow and show the company and yourself what you're truly capable of doing." And then, for the *coup de* managerial *gras*, he flips into his pseudo-expert role and tells you that this additional work is called "job enrichment," something widely viewed in management circles as a key source of enhanced motivation, satisfaction, and performance. In reality, all that has happened is that you're on the receiving end of a second job that's strikingly similar to what you're already doing. In such a transition, just about everything associated with your workload is likely to increase—except for your pay.

Your manager might call this "job enrichment," but the only enrichment going on is for your company, as a result of the elimination of one position. In fact, your manager isn't even using this term correctly. Job enrichment technically means providing an employee with more autonomy, decision-making, and managerial responsibilities in handling his or her job. Piling on more of the same work doesn't qualify as enrichment. It sounds a lot more like entombment, as your manager is smothering you with more work while showing his manager that he knows what it means to reduce overhead.

While this office idiot is relying on his watered-down comprehension of job enrichment as a rationale for placing you on the downhill side of his avalanche of chores, you need to take some action on this development, lest you end up totally buried in the morass of new work. If that happens, you're likely to be the next former employee. And pity the coworker who then gets two more jobs plopped on his or her head.

■————————————

Before you and your work suffer any further, you should meet with your manager to discuss what's going on here. First, he needs to understand that you're one person who had one job, and now you're one person who has two jobs. In a calm and businesslike manner, list the key functions that you've been fulfilling, one by one. For example, you might say, "Prior to the recent enrichment of my job, I was responsible for the following [task or tasks]. Now, with the increase in my responsibilities, I am responsible for all of that, plus [list additional tasks].” The idea behind this first salvo is to let him clearly see the sheer increase in the volume of your work.

The next step is to ask, “Would you tell me the priorities on these projects so I can be sure to complete the most important ones?” It’s okay to let him know that some of these projects are already piling up and backing up, as this will help him focus more clearly on rank-ordering what needs to be done. Once he delineates the lower priority projects, you should respond by saying, “Sounds good. Which of these latter projects can be reassigned, delegated, or deferred?” You’re not groveling and asking if any of them can possibly be shifted away from you; rather, it’s understood that some of these projects are going bye-bye. Now it’s just a matter of hearing which ones are on their way out.

Depending on how the conversation goes, there’s one more question that’s worth asking: “Because I’m handling more high-level responsibilities, what’s the plan regarding my pay for this new role?” Notice again that you’re not asking whether there’s a plan; the idea of a new payment plan is a given. You’re simply asking how it’ll work. With this question, this whole matter may end up being an enriching experience for you after all!

It’s Your Problem

Then there’s the manager who has adopted the word “empowerment” as the centerpiece of her managerial repertoire. She believes that this one word encapsulates the essence of what it means to be a manager, so she applies it to all of her dealings with her employees. Although there actually is no single strategy, approach, or philosophy that fits every situation that a manager faces, that’s not the case for office idiots. These managers hook onto a cliché or catchphrase and apply it to every issue or question that arises.

For example, let's say that all of the questions that you and your associates pose to your manager are answered with three little words: "Deal with it." If you ask any kind of follow-up, you're told, "I am empowering you to find the answer to your question." Naturally, you and your associates end up making mistakes, falling behind, and feeling frustrated.

The problem isn't that your manager expects you to solve problems on your own, but rather that this is the sole component of her managerial "strategy." Employees are capable of solving many problems on their own, and when they do so, everybody wins. In fact, the expectation that employees answer their own questions can actually build their skills, independence, and confidence. However, there's more to management than three little words, as most questions from employees call for much more than DWI, a.k.a. "deal with it." In reality, there are numerous instances when managers need to provide information, coaching, guidance, feedback, training, and hands-on support.

■────────────────────────

One strategy for dealing with this manager involves you and your associates meeting with her and letting her know that you could be far more effective and productive if she were to actually answer your questions. When you take this step, remember that she is probably asking herself, *What's in this for me?* This means that you should spell out the specific ways that she'll benefit by answering questions, rather than dodging them.

For example, you'd open your meeting with her by asking, "If we could show you a way to save time, save money, generate higher quality work, and increase output, would you be interested?" No matter how deeply entrenched she may be in the mire of office idiocy, she's still likely to say yes. Why is this important? "Yes" is one of the most powerful words in the persuasion process.

Once you get that first yes, the next step is to start spelling out the easy and time-saving steps she can take to get the positive outcomes that were so tantalizingly posed in your opening question.

Show her that all she needs to do is provide brief, clear, and factual answers to your questions. In fact, throughout this conversation, your persuasive power will be enhanced by generating numerous "yes" responses. The idea is that many little yes's along the way lead to a big yes at the end.

So how do you do this? One proven technique is to conclude your sentences with confirming questions that can generate nothing but a yes. For example, "We all want the department to work smoothly, don't we?" or "It's important to have high-quality work, isn't it?" At the same time, if your manager continues to play the DWI card, backed up with same inane claptrap about empowerment, perhaps her lack of responsiveness to your questions has nothing to do with empowerment, and everything to do with incompetence. She simply might not know the answers to your questions, and she's using empowerment as a smokescreen to keep this fact below the radar.

If she stays on this track, there's little doubt that mistakes will pile up and productivity will decline. When this becomes more apparent, one likely outcome is that someone in senior management will spot this idiocy and conclude that it's time to deal with a manager whose own credo is "Deal with it."

————————————————————————————

Not Another Team

When it comes to glomming onto marginally useful managerial trivia and tripe, it's impossible to overlook the gaggles of office idiots who are enamored with off-site teambuilding programs. These are the bouncy brigades of troopers who go off for a few days to a camp-like setting and play soldiers in paintball wars, master designers in building bridges out of toy blocks, and trapeze artists dangling from ropes. Upon returning from these harrowing adventures, the office idiot has morphed into a true believer when it comes to teams and teamwork. He thinks about teams, dreams about them, and talks of little else. If you have a question, teamwork is the answer. In fact, his fixation on teams has ironically estranged him from many of his fellow managers.

Overlooked in this process is the fact that off-site teambuilding sessions are not exactly known for their applicability to the actual workplace. In other words, while it can be fun to run around and play games with your buddies at grown-up camp, there's no reason to assume that these experiences are going to have any relevance back on the job. Not surprisingly, this fact doesn't stop an office idiot from swallowing the teamwork mantra and then returning to work and disgorging it all over his employees.

Let's take the case in which your manager has just returned from a team-building program and is totally consumed with it. As a result of his experience in an off-site playgroup, every assignment is now a team assignment. As a result, he's asked you to team up with two other employees on a project, even though you're the only one with the required expertise. You mention this to him and note that there's no need to involve the other employees. In true office idiot form, his response is that you're not a team player. Rather than rolling over to his idiotic assertion, you say something like, "I'm a team player, but just not in this case." Fresh off the heels of a teamwork indoctrination program, he replies, "That's impossible."

This simplistic black-and-white thinking is one of the hallmarks of office idiots. They grab onto a management fad or trend, and regard it as an absolute, undeniable, and unquestionable truth. Flexibility and adaptability are out, replaced by an all-or-nothing mindset that likens teamwork to a light switch that's either on or off. Of course, this type of thinking leaves these office idiots totally in the dark.

Regardless of all the quality time that your manager has wasted launching paintballs or engaging in other childish activities, he's totally missing the fact that a key element in team formation and performance is that the various skills of the members combine synergistically to move the team toward an agreed-upon goal. Since you're the only person with the requisite skills, adding two more people doesn't make this group a team; it's little more than a one-man show with two observers. Moreover, the fact that you question the very need for a team in this situation doesn't mean that you're not a team player. All that it means is that you know more about teams than your manager.

By the way, another point that has apparently escaped this office idiot is that many tasks are handled better by individuals than by teams.

Although you probably won't be able to dissuade him from his enchantment with teams, it's still worthwhile for you to talk to him about the team he has created for you. In doing so, you'd say something like, "I think teams are really important, and I want to emphasize the fact that I'm a team player. If you really want me to work on this project with both of the guys, I'll gladly do it." Notice that you opened with a clause that will immediately get him to nod in agreement. This is a quick, unspoken yes, isn't it?

At this point, you'd continue, "But as an experiment, how about if I do this particular project on my own, just this one time? If it falls short, lesson learned, and it won't happen again. And if it comes out great, then everyone wins. You get a completed project, the others can do other work, and I can do what I do best." It's a long shot with a true-believing office idiot, but it's worth a shot nonetheless. Besides, it's a variation of the trial offer, previously discussed as one of the most powerful persuasive techniques.

As a side note, the "team" that your manager is proposing would be composed of three people. In terms of group dynamics, there tend to be more interpersonal problems in groups of three than any other size. Basically, groups of three tend to morph into two-against-one scenarios. That's worth keeping in mind in the event that your manager prevails.

Either way, there's no question that teams are important in an organization, but the decision to form them should be based on reality rather than reflex.

We, We, We...

As part of the teambuilding credo, some managers buy into a related piece of advice which contends that if they use the word "we" rather than the word "I" when dealing with employees, they're likely to see increases in teamwork and camaraderie. In reality, although the occasional "royal we" from a manager can indeed send a subtle message that everyone is on the same team, excessive use of this word can have the exact opposite effect. This fact flies far above the heads of office idiots who are blithely bent on teambuilding. Given an opportunity to show that they're in the same boat as their employees, they go overboard. Figuratively, of course.

Let's look at a situation in which your manager overuses the word "we" whenever she speaks with you and your coworkers. Even when she gives you an individual assignment, she'll say that "we" need to complete it by a certain date. She also likes to check up on you and ask how "we" are doing. To say the least, it's annoying and even a wee bit confusing to be on the receiving end of this silliness.

On the one hand, many team-oriented managers occasionally use first person plural to help unite the group, build teamwork, and focus all of the players on the agreed-upon objectives. By using the word "we," a manager is letting her employees know that she's working with them as a partner, supporter, and coach. On the other hand, there's no question that too much "we" is annoying, especially if it's used in a condescending, juvenile, or parental tone. For example, just think of the tone used when a parent addresses a child with, "Now, we shouldn't be acting that way, should we?"

■————————————

When your manager's comments are making the workplace feel like a daycare center, it's time to stop toying around. You and a few of your fellow employees should meet with her to discuss this. It may be as simple as focusing on her overuse of the word "we," or there may be an array of childish treatment that needs to be addressed in conjunction with the "we" obsession.

Importantly, this discussion shouldn't be an attack on your manager. Rather, the idea is to start with something like, "We're all on the same team, and we share the same vision, values, and goals." There can be no disagreement from your manager with this opener, and notice the repeated use of the words "we" and "team," both of which obviously have a particularly positive emotional charge for her.

You'd then say, "I think we're all interested in working productively together, don't you?" An obvious yes. Then go on: "Can we talk about some aspects of our working relationship that can be even stronger?" This is a totally nonjudgmental question that opens the door to discussing any behaviors that may be interfering with the team's performance, productivity, and ability to meet its objectives. Notice that it focuses on the working relationship, and not on your manager per se.

From that point, you'd continue, "Sometimes we get confused over the use of the word 'we.' We're not sure if a project is actually assigned to us as individuals, or if we'll be working on it with each other or directly with you. This really isn't a problem as much as it is a need for a little clarification." Notice that you're clearly getting the point about the excessive use of the "royal we" onto the table, but without anything close to a direct assault. Rather, it's framed in the context of confusion more than criticism, and this makes your points easier for your manager to internalize and act upon.

Heaping on the Guilt

There's no question that a manager's expectations regarding her employees' future performance clearly influence the way they actually perform. For example, when a manager expects an employee to do an outstanding job, the likelihood of stellar performance is measurably and dramatically increased. Conversely, when a manager expects an employee to flop, the odds of tanking skyrocket. The primary reason is that managers telegraph their expectations to their employees, who then internalize these expectations and act accordingly.

At issue here is the flighty flock of office idiots who know enough to articulate positive expectations to their employees, but then taint these expectations with weird consequences if such expectations are not met. One of the more common varieties of this weirdness is demonstrated by idiotic managers who broadcast upbeat expectations, and then play the guilt card in describing the consequences of less-than-satisfactory performance.

For example, take the case in which your manager sets positive expectations for you and your team when doling out assignments, especially through such comments as, "I know it's demanding, but I know you guys can do it." However, the kicker comes when he adds how disappointed he'll be if things don't come out so well, such as by saying, "I'll be personally hurt if you come up short on this." And then, if the project does miss the mark, he harps on how you failed him and how he expected so much more of you. This manager's style is best described as "management by guilt." You can almost hear him say, "Is that what you want to do to me? I work so hard every day, and this is the thanks I get?"

His managerial style is highly egocentric. Instead of focusing on the ways in which subpar performance will impact goal attainment, commitments, or deadlines, he's more concerned about how it'll impact him. He's operating under the assumption that you'll be more energized to work hard if you believe that less-than-excellent performance is going to hurt him and make him feel upset and disappointed. Perhaps this would be a normal reaction if he were making a special dinner that you might not like, but such thinking belongs in the kitchen, not in the workplace.

Rather than allowing his positive expectations to be an inspiration, the guilt trip that he attaches to them make them a distraction. After all, when considering some of the most powerful motivators at work, such as achievement, recognition, personal growth, responsibility, and advancement, it's abundantly evident that guilt doesn't exactly have a place on this list.

This situation calls for you and some of your associates to have a little chat with this office idiot, but not immediately. Rather, the best time to talk to him about his combo plate of positive expectations and family-sized buckets of guilt is after you've completed a project successfully.

At such a time, you'd open the conversation with positive comments about the upbeat expectations that he has established for each of you and the team, along with comments about the success of the most recent project. You'd add, "But we're not sure if we can reach this type of outcome again," and then stop talking. This sentence is an intentional attention-grabber that's designed to shock him and cause him to focus on what you're about to say. You'd then wrap up by saying, "To be successful going down the road, we think we can work more effectively with you if we all focus on the goals and the strategies that are needed to meet them, rather than on the idea of not disappointing you. And don't worry. We're not going to disappoint you. You give us a lot of encouragement and support, and that's all we need. What do you think?"

Notice that you're not criticizing him or making any demands. Rather, you're simply suggesting ways that all of you can work more productively and successfully together by focusing more on results and less on remorse. Importantly, you wrap up your comments with a question that invites his input, and by doing so, you're increasing the palatability and impact of your message.

Loosey Goosey

Many office idiots who struggle with the art of management flail about in an unending quest for the one best way to manage. Naturally, there are pontificators out there who may preach about one strategy or another that they believe is the penultimate method to manage the troops. Unfortunately, there's madness to such methods. *There simply isn't one best way to manage.* Management is highly situational, as there are some instances in which a manager will need to take direct, forceful, and unilateral actions, while other scenarios call for a manager to engage in far less direct involvement and guidance. Such factors as the skill mix of the employees, the timing of the situation at hand, and the magnitude of the required resources all play a role in determining which managerial approach will be the best fit.

In spite of this, and in an attempt to make management simpler—a rather predictable goal for office idiots—some managers blithely opt for a strategy in which employees are granted huge amounts of autonomy, independence, and freedom. The office idiots who embrace this strategy often justify their lack of leadership over their reports by claiming that autonomy is the best way to demonstrate trust in one's employees, while also building their skills, self-esteem, and decision-making abilities. Of course, what these office idiots are really doing is simply ignoring their responsibilities as managers and turning all of their direct reports loose. This isn't management; it's abdication.

Let's take a situation in which your manager has been granted total autonomy by her manager. Rather than seeing monumental growth in her skills, decision-making, and self-esteem, all you're actually seeing is that she's doing the minimal amount of work every day, while passing huge amounts of time on personal calls and the Internet. She occasionally emerges from her office, dumps some work on you and your associates, and then returns to her personal business. Her manager, a true believer in managerial autonomy, is aware of her antics, but he doesn't seem to care. This surprisingly common situation is the perfect corporate storm. Namely, it's a manager who gives his employee the freedom to do whatever she wants, and an employee who freely wants to do nothing. As an employee in this type of situation, you've got to wonder why your manager's manager would allow this to happen. Clearly, it's a matter of office idiocy for him to tolerate this. However, if you look behind the scenes, there can be any number of idiotic explanations.

For example, some managers let this happen simply because they're incompetent. They may toss around terms like "autonomy," but they're clueless when it comes to managing anything. Other managers opt for this loose strategy because they want to be liked by their employees. They're afraid to say no because their employees might not like them anymore. So, they toss the reins aside and let the troops run wild. Of course, they don't understand that employees don't particularly like managers who don't manage. The truth is that employees would rather report to bona fide managers who treat them with respect and trust, while providing them with challenging assignments supported by feedback and guidance when needed.

In addition, there are the managerial idiots who let individual employees get away with questionable behaviors because of favoritism, a family or personal connection, or a "special situation." After all, you do not have to look too far to find situations in which a manager and employee have more than a casual working relationship. It's also possible that a free-range employee has some damaging information about the manager, and the only way to keep it from going viral is to let this employee go feral.

Amazingly enough, there are also many managers who let employees do whatever they want in order to avoid expending the time, energy, effort, and dollars associated with finding, hiring, and orienting a replacement. The trademarks of these office idiots include laziness, inertia, and slovenliness.

■————————————————————

The prescription for dealing with this type of situation is a little tricky. If you go to your direct manager and express concern about her preference for personal calls and the Internet over doing her job, you're not likely to get a warm response. And if you go to her manager, the great abdicator who has enabled your manager's ridiculous behaviors in the first place, you're again destined to encounter a rather inhospitable reaction. However, there are two possible options for you to consider—one is the next rung on the corporate ladder, and the other is the Human Resources department, if your organization has one. Importantly, if you sit in silence on this matter, one outcome is guaranteed: it isn't going to change. In fact, it's likely to get worse, if that's possible.

When you and a few of your associates meet with a more senior member of management or the HR manager or director, make sure your comments are clear, specific, behaviorally based, and verifiable. For example: "We're really concerned about what's going on in our department, and we believe that there's a situation that's putting all of the employees and even the company at risk. May we talk to you in confidence about this?" Assuming that your comments will be treated as confidential, you'd then focus on specific examples of questionable behaviors that directly contradict the company's performance standards and expectations. You may add, "We don't expect you to take any action based on what we're saying, other than to please investigate this matter for yourself. If you want to conduct an anonymous survey of the entire department, that would be even better. All we're saying is that we're trying to do our jobs and do our best for the company, but the leadership situation over there is preventing it."

———————————————————————■

Unless your organization is widely infected with the abdication bug, this situation will soon be out in the open, and at least two managers are going to have to do something rather than nothing.

9

OFFICE IDIOTS AND THEIR IDIOTIC FEEDBACK

Effective feedback in the workplace is one of the foundational building blocks of employee communication, motivation, and performance. When feedback is mishandled, the door is left wide open for mistakes, missed deadlines, frustration, dissatisfaction, resentment, complaints, and disgust—to name just a few of the damages that asinine feedback generates. Not surprisingly, when it comes to delivering fatuous feedback, there are no better purveyors than office idiots. Given a chance to subvert the entire feedback process, office idiots are always ready to serve. Although they're not prepared to do much at work, this is definitely in their repertoire.

Instant Criticism

One of the more common displays of office idiocy in the feedback arena is demonstrated daily by managers whose standard operating procedure is to criticize whatever the employees do, and to do so without even pausing for a nanosecond to see if this instant negativity is warranted.

Let's say that you're one of the unfortunate souls who submit reports or analyses to this kind of manager, only to find that he starts criticizing your work before it even arrives. In his narrow and negative world, employees are always wrong. When you initially submit work to him, whether in person or online, his only response should be an acknowledgement that your work is in his hands.

Before figuring out how to deal with this brand of idiocy, it's helpful to take a couple of steps back and consider the reasons why a manager would instantly criticize work he hasn't even seen. Such behavior is an obvious and automatic sign that other issues are interfering with the manager's objectivity, professionalism, and overall managerial skills. Some managers do this kind of thing because they're grossly insecure and fearful that the expertise and prowess of their employees will come through in these projects and outshine their own. Therefore, to keep their status and stature in the company, they instantly react negatively to their employees' work.

⸻

The best way to deal with an office idiot who'd rather "no" than "know" is to have a sit-down session where you and some of your associates discuss ways to improve the working relationship. One key point that will help you open and initially steer this meeting is to say something like this: "We're concerned that some potentially successful ideas may be getting sidelined because they're not being fully considered. What can we do to increase the likelihood that our analyses, reports, and comments will get more time and attention?" Notice that you didn't use the word "you," and you posed your comments as a question for him to answer, rather than as an accusation that would lead to a defensive reaction from him. In response to your question, he may give you some tips regarding the ways he'd like you to present information to him.

A related strategy is essentially a workplace "instant replay." With this strategy, you'd say to your manager, "Can you tell us about the times when employees submitted reports and analyses or made comments that really hit the mark? What did they do that we're not doing?" He's likely to tell you about a few employees somewhere, perhaps some time ago, whose work grabbed his attention. When he tells you how they got through to him, your next step is to follow their example.

———————————————————————————————■

Minimizing and Trivializing

Not only are there masses of office idiots who reject their employees' work sight unseen, but there are just as many who will review whatever their employees produce but still respond with a putdown. Regardless of the actual quality of the work, these office idiots are always armed and ready to launch a salvo of insults, criticism, and trash talk.

Let's look at a situation in which your manager subscribes to a philosophy of management by disparagement. When you wrap up a project, she always makes a degrading remark about it. She appears to be particularly comfortable telling you that your work isn't important. This common commentary sets a framework for her to automatically denigrate your work. For example, even if you've done an amazing, outstanding, and incredible job, your manager has already framed it as unimportant. It's as if you spent your time counting the blades of grass on the lawn. Even if you did an amazing job, it's unimportant, so who cares? It's a classic no-win situation. If you do an exceptional job as a grass counter, it means nothing. And if you happen to miss a few blades, then you didn't even do your insignificant job well. Of course, the problem is that your work is significant and important. Just not in your manager's eyes.

Interestingly, if your manager believes that your work is insignificant, she's actually making a negative statement about herself as a manager. After all, you presumably receive your assignments from her, and if she emphasizes how insignificant they are, one can only wonder about her ability to identify and assign meaningful work. In addition, if she's always ready to trash-talk the quality or quantity of your work, all she's doing is raising more questions about her managerial skills. If she were engaging in effective managerial behaviors, including the practice of managing by wandering around (MBWA), this problematic outcome would likely never occur. By communicating regularly with the employees and providing ongoing coaching, guidance, and follow-up along the way, the most likely outcome is that crises are averted, quality is high, and goals are met.

■————————————————

Because your manager is either uninterested or incapable of seeing and appreciating your accomplishments, one basic step is for you to document them. This literally means spelling out the details of your key achievements, including the project's title, dates, actions, results, and measurable benefits to the department and company at large. With this documentation in place, your next step is actually several steps, and they all lead directly to your manager's office and a meeting with her. Your goal is to let her see what you've been doing and accomplishing. However, if you simply walk into her office and dump this on her, she may go into stimulus overload and hear nothing.

As a result, the best way to frame this meeting is to tell your manager something like, "I'd like to meet with you to clarify my objectives for the coming year. I want to make sure that my goals are in sync with yours, and I'm interested in any additional goals that you have in mind for me." Most managers are not going to turn away employees who want to work with them to establish, clarify, and enhance their goals. In this meeting, the first step is to review all of the goals that you've met during the past year, and then use this as a springboard to establish your goals for the coming year.

This strategy has all sorts of advantages. It lets your manager truly see how important your job is, how successful you've been in meeting or exceeding your goals, and how motivated you are to establish even more challenging goals for the coming year. In addition, with your manager playing an active role in your goal-setting process, she'll be far less likely to say that they're unimportant—that would be tantamount to saying that her ideas are unimportant, and most office idiots aren't *that* idiotic.

Looking down the road, you should keep your manager updated when you hit the established benchmarks or meet key objectives. Importantly, when you provide such information, it shouldn't be in the form of a boast, but rather as a factual update that enumerates what you've done and the benefits that have accrued as a result. Besides, your numerous accomplishments also reflect positively on her as manager, and that's certainly important to her.

Crushing Creativity

A close cousin of the "no-it-all" manager is the office idiot who regards creative thinking—a.k.a. cool ideas beyond whatever is required to merely do the job—as a cardinal offense that must be deterred. This manager's mantra is "Leave well enough alone," even if well enough isn't good enough. To this manager's way of thinking, an employee's job is to do his or her assigned tasks and leave the creativity, innovation, and insights to someone else. This is the office idiot who's fully committed to thinking inside the box.

Let's say that you're in the unenviable position of reporting to one of these idiots. He has made it abundantly clear that he has no interest in your ideas and suggestions. Whenever you mention one to him, he responds with such pat phrases as "Just do your job," "It's not as simple as that," or "That failed when we tried it before."

If you want a shot at opening your manager's eyes, ears, and mind, the first place to look is actually at the ideas that you've been presenting. In a word, are they arguably intelligible, or are they so off-the-wall as to generate an "Oh, no—not again!" not only from your manager, but from anyone within listening distance? If your ideas really are long on content, creativity, and utility, yet they are still subjected to instant rejection, then it's a matter of applying some creative strategies to help your manager see that it's okay to look forward rather than backward.

First, spell out the benefits that will result from your ideas, such as by showing your manager how they can reduce costs, save money, enhance productivity, improve service, upgrade quality, energize the team, build satisfaction, or increase profits. This isn't a time for painting with broad strokes, but for getting right down to the detailed points in each of these areas. In fact, if this were a painting, it would be pointillism.

Your manager may be receptive to going with a trial period, in which you ask him to use the next 30 days to drop his input-deflecting shield and actually solicit employee ideas, discuss them, tweak them, and give the better ones a try. If, at the end of this period, he finds that these ideas do not deliver the goods, he can set this experiment aside and return to the world of Paleolithic management. However, if some arguably strong ideas are generated during the trial period, then this approach is no longer a trial. Period.

A related strategy is to ask him to consider a brainstorming session for the department. In such a gathering, all of the participants are totally free to make any suggestions that could help the department. There's no criticism, and no such thing as a dumb idea. After all, an idea that appears to be totally dopey can give someone another idea, and that can generate still another, and soon enough, some amazing innovations can come to life.

———————————————————————■

The value of such a session is that it'll help your manager see that a more open and receptive work atmosphere can generate great results that lead to better performance, better products, and better morale (and, by the way, better recognition for him). There's also the possibility that this type of experience will be the "Ah-ha" moment that takes him to a higher level of managerial understanding, far above the haze of idiocy that is blurring his ability to see what effective management really means. After all, just as attitudes shape behaviors, it's also true that behaviors shape attitudes. If your manager can truly experience what it means to foster creative thinking, perhaps his attitude toward such thinking will change.

Leaving Matters Up in the Air

Office idiots not only stumble when it comes to the content, method, and style of their feedback; they're also well known for selecting the worst possible venues in which to dole it out. Some of the resoundingly unsuitable locales include restaurants, hotel lobbies, break rooms, and airport lounges. And speaking of airports, some office idiots are so flighty that they regard the flights themselves as primo sites for employee feedback.

Let's assume that you report to one of those airheaded managers who believe that a five-hour flight across the country is an opportune time for some feedback. As you buckle up, she says that she wants to use this opportunity to give you your performance review. You pull the buckle a little tighter, since this could be a bumpy ride.

Airplanes are great for many things, but a performance evaluation isn't one of them. This type of evaluation should be a private discussion in which you and your manager freely and openly discuss your performance and candidly express ideas, opinions, concerns, and suggestions. None of this belongs in a public venue, whether on the ground or in the air. Having an audience in close proximity eliminates any chance of a real dialogue, especially in terms of the coaching and candor necessary in any decent performance appraisal. And it's even worse when the audience includes everyone within five rows of you, plus the screaming child across the aisle, plus the passenger who's trying to pull out his carry-on bag that's stored in the bin directly above you.

Furthermore, performance appraisals should be free of interruptions, and that certainly isn't the case when in flight. In addition to the beverage service and people nearby who need to use the restrooms, there are all sorts of announcements, such as those concerning the sights below, the movie services, and, uh-oh, the turbulence ahead. And speaking of turbulence, it's extremely difficult to focus on any kind of feedback when the plane is being tossed like a salad. And even worse when your salad ends up in your lap. Even the seating configuration on an airplane is all wrong for a feedback session. When a manager and employee meet for a performance appraisal, they should sit face-to-face so that they can capture all of the nuances of the communication process, including facial expressions, body positioning, and even tone.

Airplanes can be rather noisy, and many of the subtleties of the spoken word are lost in the din.

When you report to a manager who thinks that it's okay to conduct a performance appraisal in this type of setting, someone actually needs to evaluate her performance, especially when it comes to handling performance evaluations.

The best way to deal with an office idiot who has set his sights on airborne evaluations is to stop the process before it starts. You can put the kibosh on this idiocy by being totally honest and saying, "I'm really interested in getting feedback from you, and I've been looking forward to this discussion. But in all honesty, with everything going on during a flight, it's going to be really hard for me to concentrate on what you'll be saying. I think I'll gain a lot more from this if we can do it on the ground and in private. If you'll just say when and where, and I'll be there."

Hopefully, your manager will come to understand that performance evaluations should be well-grounded in every sense of the word.

Are You Talking to Me?

Looking further at feedback that's provided in performance appraisals, one of the most prevalent practices of office idiots is to surprise their employees in the evaluation process, typically by providing low ratings when the employees were anticipating glowing reviews. On the eve of such an evaluation, some of these managers will lament, "I don't want to do this review tomorrow because my employee is expecting all high scores, and I have to tell her that she's doing poorly." Of course, the one person who's actually performing poorly in this scenario is the manager.

Let's say you're expecting a very positive review, only to have your performance absolutely hammered during the evaluation session. One of your manager's main points is that you need to work on your attitude. The first and biggest problem here is that there should never be any surprises in a performance appraisal session. If your manager is doing her job—that is, providing you with ongoing coaching, guidance, feedback, and support during the evaluation period—both of you will already know how you're doing when the time comes for a more formal evaluation. Rather than being a shocker, this session establishes the formal documentation of your performance during the evaluation period, while also setting the stage for your goals for the coming period.

In addition, for real learning to occur, feedback should be provided as soon as possible after the behavior in question. Your manager fails on this point, too. Your manager also gets a "needs improvement" when it comes to the kind of feedback that she provides. Feedback that's overly general is meaningless, and there's no better example than telling an employee that he or she has a "questionable attitude." What does that even mean? Is it arguing? Tardiness? Sloppiness? Laziness? Who knows.

———■———————————————————

If your manager wants to provide feedback regarding your attitude, it's essential for her to phrase it in terms of what's measurable—performance, behaviors, outcomes, and results. And that's where you need to focus in order to pull your evaluation out of the realm of meaningless idiocy. In doing so, you should meet with her and say, "I understand that you're concerned about my attitude, and I really want to improve. To help me do this, can you please give me examples of any of my behaviors or performance that reflect a questionable attitude?" If your manager had been doing her job, she would have already advised you about such behaviors during the course of her MBWA. There would have been no shock during the review process, and it's likely that you would have already corrected the behaviors that led to this negative assessment in the first place.

Nonetheless, if your manager pulls a few unrelated incidents out of her dunce hat and indicates that they're examples of your attitudinal problems, be sure to hear her out. It's very easy to become defensive when receiving such feedback, but if you remain calm and listen, you'll be showing her respect and gaining insight into the kinds of behaviors that she links to higher performance ratings. Even if her examples are totally out of line, you shouldn't jump all over her during this session. Rather, gather all of your supportive data, and then ask to meet with her again under the auspices of trying to fully understand exactly what she expects of you going forward. In this second session, present her with your factual data, and then see what she has to say.

At the very least, she'll understand that you're not going to roll over when she pulls labels out of thin air. And at best, she may actually get some accurate insight into you and your performance.

He Said, She Said

There are packs of idiotic managers who are quick to provide negative feedback based on a combination of limited data and stilted input from others. These managers are easily influenced by whoever gets to them first, and they are quick to take action. It may be the wrong action, but it's swift, and that's all that matters to them.

Take the situation in which you provide fair and accurate feedback to two of your employees, but they disagree with what you say. You review the facts with them, and you jointly establish plans to help them improve. Apparently this isn't good enough for either of them. They get together and complain to your manager. Instantly believing everything they say, he calls you into his office and criticizes you. Unreceptive to your input and perspective on what happened, he simply states that you need to maintain a better working relationship with your team.

It's ironic that your manager would comment on your relationship with your team, given that his relationship with at least one member of his team—you—is less than stellar. If you really want to know what he's doing, it's called *projecting*. He's simply taking one of his weaknesses (his inability to work well with his employees) and projecting it onto you.

There are at least two other causal factors behind your manager's idiotic position in this situation. The first one is that managers who undercut their direct reports in this way are often too interested in being liked by the rank and file. These managers believe that if they kowtow to the whims of the troops, they'll be beloved. As noted previously, managers who flop over like this don't realize that they come across as weak, tractable, and insecure. The second factor behind your manager's swift and ill-conceived action is that he wants to show your employees that he's the boss and, by golly, he means business. When employees come and talk to him, things are going to happen. By instantly jumping on you, he believes that he is acting as a decisive, responsive, and powerful leader. In reality, he's simply a poster boy for office idiocy.

Digging himself even deeper in his own morass of idiocy, your manager chastises you solely on the basis of what your employees say, while totally blocking your comments and rebuttal. At best, this means that he only had half the facts when he drew his conclusion. On a scale of one to 10, he gets a five—a failing grade. A non-idiotic manager, on the other hand, would have dealt quite differently with your two dissidents. He or she would have listened carefully to what they had to say, encouraged them to deal directly with you on this matter, and then discussed their concerns with you.

This type of situation cries out for a follow-up meeting between you and your manager. The objective is quite simple: to provide all of the facts supporting the feedback that you provided to the two employees in question, and to establish a strategy to prevent a repeat performance of the current situation.

One of the better ways to set up such a meeting is to say, "I know you're a fair person who likes to make decisions based on full and accurate information, and I'm wondering when we can meet to fill in some of the blanks regarding a couple of my employees who met with you." Notice that this request opens with a complimentary phrase that can only generate agreement and pride from your manager, followed by a soft question that automatically assumes that the two of you will be meeting to discuss what happened here. In this second clause, you're not asking *if* you both can meet, but *when*. Also, notice the light and conversational tone. By avoiding an overly formal approach, you're setting the tone for a conversation, not a confrontation. And finally, note that there's no mention of your manager's idiotic actions. You'll get nowhere fast if you head down that path.

In the meeting itself, your initial goal is to provide your manager with the facts behind the negative feedback that you gave to your employees. You're not out to blast them for running to him, nor are you out to blast him for excluding you from the process. Ideally, as you provide him with compelling information, he's going to draw his own conclusions about the information that your two employees provided. If he can get there on his own, rather than through your coaxing and cajoling, it's far more likely to stick.

The final goal is to look forward and jointly establish a strategy to prevent this type of problem from occurring again in the future. For example, you'd say, "Going down the road, if any of my employees do this again, I think the best way to handle it is to get me involved immediately. I have no problem with any of them coming to you—in fact, I encourage it—and I want to be able to come to you, too."

It's a Scream

One of the most common forms of idiotic feedback comes at outrageously high-decibel levels. This is the feedback from managers who yell and scream whenever things don't go the way they want or expect. They're uniquely qualified to transform any work situation into a scream-fest. Their ability to tolerate frustration is zero, and ironically, most of their employees have about the same level of tolerance toward their outbursts.

For example, take the case in which your manager is capable of functioning within the realm of normalcy—that is, until something goes wrong. At that instant, rather than reacting with a well-reasoned and measured response, he flips immediately into rage mode and yells and screams at you and your associates. One question runs through the minds of everyone within earshot of his eruptions, namely, *If this manager can't manage himself, how in the world can he manage anyone else?* And the answer to that question is, of course, "Not well."

It's unacceptable to work in a department where the manager is a stick of dynamite, and everyone else is a match. After all, as an employee you're allowed to make mistakes. You're even allowed to fail. In fact, if you're not making mistakes, you're not learning. However, when you report to a screamer, you're constantly walking on eggshells. If employees are afraid to make a mistake because their manager will go Vesuvian, they become immobilized, sensing that they can be subjected to a brutal verbal assault at any time. This is a true manifestation of the expression "petrified with fear." Obviously, under these circumstances, there's no chance that anyone will go the extra mile, unless it's to get away from this manager.

———

When dealing with this corporate powder keg, it's essential to refrain from taking his outbursts personally. If you get caught in the crosshairs of his cross words, it would not be surprising for you to experience self-doubt and self-recrimination, thinking somehow that this is all your fault. Well, it's not. Your manager's outbursts are due to his problems, not yours.

You should also avoid the temptation to fire back at him when he launches a barrage of enraged comments at you. In his state of mind, the notion of listening to others is simply not on the menu. In fact, any actions that you take to calm him down are likely to drag you deeper into the melee, generate increasingly vitriolic verbal abuse, and further inflame the situation. When he goes off like this, your best bet is to go off somewhere else.

There are a few strategies that can help you work with someone like this. For example, by carefully observing your manager's behavior, you may be able to identify some of the factors that trigger his tantrums. Perhaps he's set off by typos, messy offices, tardiness, interruptions, delays, or criticism. Whatever it may be, if you can identify some of the issues that throw him into a fit, perhaps you can work around or avoid them before the trigger is pulled. In addition, because there are calm periods between even the most violent storms, you and some of your fellow employees should use one of these lulls as an opportunity to meet with this manager and talk to him about his screaming. However, you'll need to tread carefully here, especially if you've already identified constructive criticism as one of his triggers.

If you feel it's safe to approach him about his outbursts, the idea would be to say something like, "We don't know what to do about a problem that's tearing the department apart. It's hurting us and everything that we do. Productivity. Quality. Morale. Loyalty." Then stop talking. His interest will be piqued, and he'll inquire further. When he does, you'd respond by saying, "It's the yelling and screaming. We want to help. Just tell us how." Notice that this approach isn't an attack on him personally. Rather, your comments open with a genuine work-oriented concern about departmental performance, and by pausing after the opening statement, your manager is drawn into the dialogue. In fact, with this approach, he opens the door to the topic himself. Your comments then wrap up with a respectful request for his thoughts on how to handle this matter, rather than with some parental advice from you.

It won't take much time for you to determine if this approach has any traction. If you find that your manager didn't get your message, you should seek out someone in senior management or human resources who will.

10

POWER-TRIPPING OFFICE IDIOTS

There are legions of office idiots who are freakishly obsessed with exerting control over people and situations. They're known companywide as control freaks.

Some of their trademark behaviors include taking over conversations, topping whatever others say, insisting that everything be done their way, boasting about every conceivable topic, degrading the accomplishments of others, virtually shoving everyone else around, and having all of the answers—even when there are no questions. In constant pursuit of opportunities to flex their power over anyone who strays into their airspace, they apply a vast array of controlling strategies, from subtle to over-the-top. And there's no reason to assume that they're only at the top of an organization. Power-seeking jerks are ensconced at every level. They can be managers. They can be peers. They can even be direct reports.

That Pesky Final Word

One of the most common behaviors displayed by hyper-controlling office idiots is a freaky fixation on having the last word. Not a single conversation, discussion, or disagreement can end until these jerks have made a final comment. They have to be the period at the end of every sentence. Period.

A particularly trying and frying experience for any employee is to report to one of these idiots. Let's assume that you're in that unfortunate position. Whenever you have a difference of opinion with your manager, whether in person or in an e-mail, she keeps pushing until she has the last word, even if she's clearly wrong.

In dealing with this type of office idiot, one strategy that won't work is to engage in a verbal sparring match in which you try to land the last punch line. Any card-carrying office idiot will keep launching verbal blows until you finally give in. Besides, you've got to be extra careful about pushing a pushy manager to the brink. Not only is she going to hold her ground, but she's also likely to hold this incident against you.

When confronted with an unbending control freak who's bent on having the final word (one that is far removed from reality), there are a couple of techniques that will help balance the scales. For starters, you'll need to base your comments on clear, specific, and measurable facts. However, that might not be enough. It's very easy for control freaks to simply deny the facts or make up their own. If that happens, you'll need to take your facts to the next level, and that's accomplished by linking them to what is called *source credibility*. People are more likely to believe information if it comes from people they trust.

With that in mind, if certain individuals or organizations are near and dear to your over-controlling manager's heart, package your facts with an endorsement or testimonial from one of them. For example, you'd say, "I understand, and that's a good point, and so-and-so looked at this same matter and said such-and-such about it." After you've cited so-and-so, a totally credible source, at least for your manager, and expressed that person's views on the matter at hand, stop talking. A classic idiotic manager is likely to go with one of two responses. The first one is typically, "I'm not so sure about that, but I'm going to check it out." In response, you simply say, "Okay." The discussion ends then and there—and look who had the final word!

———————————————————————————————■

A second common reaction when an over-controlling office idiot is confronted with contradictory information from one of her idols is for her to switch into trivializing mode and diminish the significance of the entire discussion. With this tactic, she's likely to say, "Whatever. It doesn't matter anyhow." This response is nothing but a rationalization. Your controlling manager knows that she has lost her war of last words, and her only way to cope is to pretend that the issue itself wasn't important. By making the issue insignificant, the control freak rests comfortably with the belief that it makes no difference who had the last word. Thus, her ego remains intact as she eagerly scours the landscape for another opportunity to have the final word.

As a side note, if she continues to find that she simply can't have the last word with you, that can have a lasting impact on her.

Who Made You the Boss?

From an organizational standpoint, employees are supposed to receive assignments, projects, and directives from their manager or supervisor. However, that fact somehow escapes another motley mob of office idiots, the power-playing peers who are always ready to step in and tell their coworkers what they should be doing. Importantly, these are not your friendly and collaborative coworkers who want to share ideas with you about projects that may help the department or company. Rather, we're talking about power-seeking coworkers who think they're your boss. They're not interested in helping the department or the company; they're only interested in helping themselves.

Take the case in which one of these power-seekers keeps telling you about additional projects, chores, or tasks that you should be completing. There's nothing about this person's role, responsibility, or title that includes foisting work on you, but he's delighted to do so. You're not so delighted.

From the outset, the key point to remember is that the only way he can have power over you is for you to give it to him. If you establish a pattern of doing whatever he demands, you'll be rewarding his bossy behavior, and that means he's going to continue to play the power card. However, if you stop playing serf, he'll stop playing lord.

At the same time, this doesn't mean that you need to be nasty, mean, or aggressive. Just be clear, direct, and businesslike. You can say something as basic as, "Thanks for the suggestions. I've checked them out, but I really won't be doing anything with them."

Even with this brief response, there are a couple of interesting points to note. First, aside from the thanks (which is all the reinforcement that he'll be getting from you for this little escapade), notice that you called his directives "suggestions." Lest he think that he's somehow presenting you with orders or guidelines, this is a subtle way of telling him exactly how you calibrate his input. Second, notice also that you say that you "won't" be using his suggestions. This is a contraction for "will not," indicating that you're unwilling to go with whatever he's suggesting. This wording is very different from saying that you "can't" use his suggestions, as "can't" means that you lack the ability to do so. Clearly, you've got the ability, but you don't have the willingness, interest, time, need, or desire to go one step further with any of this.

What You Don't Know

While jockeying for the last word in every discussion is an example of a controlling behavior that's in your face, other controlling behaviors are played out behind your back. This positioning makes it much easier for office idiots to stab you in the back.

For example, let's say you have an employee who withholds important information from you. When your manager asks you about projects in this employee's domain, you're missing some of data, so he calls her instead. When you confront her and ask why she didn't provide you with all of the information in the first place, she says something like, "Well, you didn't ask for it."

Before defining a strategy to deal with this type of office idiot, let's dig a little deeper and see why she might be doing this in the first place. When employees pull these kinds of stunts, the root causes are usually power and control needs. These needs, in turn, are usually accompanied by a few other self-serving motivators. For example, employees who willfully hoard information are also demonstrating a strong need for attention. If they can look good in front of their manager's manager, they can put halos on themselves and horns on you. The outcome of this tactic is that your employee appears to be on top of her game, while you appear to be on top of the dumpster.

With this conniving approach, you can see that your employee is also playing another card that's closely associated with power, the political card. She's showing the shrewdness and deceitfulness that personifies many underhanded political operatives whose objective is to set fairness, honesty, and ethics aside in an unwavering pursuit of self-aggrandizement.

Your employee also uses a highly manipulative tactic in responding to your question about the information she held back. She innocently contends that the onus is on you to ask for it, and if you don't, it's fair game for her to withhold this card and play it later if she's asked by someone else (your manager, for example). As a power-seeking office idiot, she knows that information is power. And by withholding facts, figures, or data from you, her goal is to take power from your arsenal and place it firmly in hers. And if she can flash her knowledge in front of your manager at your expense, it's a home run for her. And a strikeout for you.

———————————————

Two key strategies are particularly effective in countering her little power game. One is for you to be more of a grand inquisitor when you meet with her to discuss her work. Extra use of open-ended questions that start with who, what, where, when, why, and how should be on your menu from start to finish. However, as a power hungry office idiot, your employee may still figure out how to hold back a few gems. So, you should always wrap up the discussion by asking, "This has all been very helpful. Now, are there any questions that I should have asked, but didn't?"

To help soften its bite, this type of inquiry opens with a supportive and complimentary comment, but it still forces the issue. If she fails to bring out any intel on matters that ultimately cause your manager to go to her, her power-playing office idiocy jumps to center stage for all to see. And her claim that you failed to ask her about the issue in question goes right down the drain. There's also a firmer and more direct approach to consider. Instead of tweaking your inquiries, you can address this matter head-on for what it really is—insubordination. Your employee's behavior is right out of the insubordinate's handbook in that it reeks of disrespect, fails to follow managerial directives, and includes a sprinkling of defiance.

As a result, you have the option of reprimanding her for insubordination. The process starts with a verbal warning, and it would be provided in a closed-door session just with her. You'd say something like, "On a number of occasions, including such-and-such a date, you withheld key information in our discussions. I have mentioned my concern about this matter to you several times in the past, and I'm now doing so formally. I want you to understand that if the problem continues, I will take more severe disciplinary action, and that may include termination. I'll be placing a note in your file indicating that we had this conversation today, and my real hope is that we can move forward with far more open communication."

She may be inclined to hold back information, but these comments clearly show that you're not.

Power Grabbing

Pushing the envelope a little further, there are power-grabbing office idiots whose appetite for control isn't satisfied by merely holding back information from their managers. These jerks hunger for more, and they have no qualms about devouring some of their managers' responsibilities.

Let's say that you have one of these piranhas reporting to you, incessantly ripping off pieces of your job. He has no problem assigning projects to himself that are clearly your responsibility, to the point of meeting with other managers regarding issues that fall under your umbrella, and even contacting vendors regarding services associated with your job. When you speak to him about these idiotic antics, he gets huffy, denies the problem, claims he's actually helping you, and then says that there's really nothing to discuss.

In the first place, this employee needs to understand that he has a job to do, and it's his, not yours. There's no reason to let him continue to grab your responsibilities just because he goes into denial when you discuss these actions with him. Playing the huffy card is simply part of his power-playing repertoire; it's a tool to stop a discussion in its tracks and provide an opening for him to head back to his lair. And as for his comment about helping you, he only wants to help one person—himself.

When you have one of these power players salivating over the next chunk of your job that he'll consume, it's time to reassert your control. First, take a careful and thorough look at what he has actually been doing, especially his central responsibilities and the extent to which he's been successfully carrying them out. After all, how can he be doing anything close to a good job while taking over parts of yours? Odds are, you'll see that his assigned responsibilities are suffering. If this is the case, you should provide him with clear and specific feedback regarding every shortfall you find. You should also discuss and agree upon specific steps that he'll need to take in order to bring his work back to acceptable levels.

You should also review the components of your job that he has purloined and let him see the shortcomings of his work in this area, as well. For example, you'd say, "When you go off on your own and take on responsibilities that are mine, we end up with duplicated efforts, miscommunication, confusion, errors, and wasted time and money. For example, let's look at what happened when you took on such-and-such project without my knowledge or approval." At that point, give him a blow-by-blow description of the ways in which his unilateral actions on this project created significant measurable problems for you, your department, and even the company at large.

The next step is to provide him with a bullet-point listing of his responsibilities, along with an unequivocal directive that he's to focus only in these areas. If he's interested in any additional work beyond the scope of this list, it must be approved by you in advance.

Conclude your discussion by advising him of the possible consequences associated with ignoring you on this matter. Frankly, he needs to understand that further performance issues of this sort can lead to termination. If he continues to let his performance slide and unilaterally assume your responsibilities, you can unilaterally assume that he's willing to face those consequences.

By Any Other Name

One of the more common power plays executed by managerial office idiots is to affix nicknames to their employees. On the surface, this doesn't sound like much of a power play. For power-playing jerks, that's the beauty of this tactic.

A person's name is one of the most emotionally charged words that he or she knows. When people hear their name, there's a physical and mental reaction that is qualitatively different from the way they react to any other sound. A person's name has strong psychological underpinnings, to the point of virtually defining who he or she is. Addressing an employee by a nickname is a way to trivialize his or her name, and thereby trivialize the employee, as well.

Who gets to bestow nicknames on others? The answer is the person with the most power. In the nomenclature game, employees don't get to affix nicknames to their managers—certainly not in the way that managers can unilaterally assign them to their subordinates. Nicknames that emanate from the troops are often less-than-flattering monikers that are only uttered when the manager is out of earshot.

Let's look at a scenario in which you report to a nicknaming manager. He bestows nicknames on whoever works for him, and just to make sure there's no question as to where the power lies, all of these appellations are different animals. He seemingly doles out these names in fun, but could it be that the real message is that he is the ringmaster, and the employees are his tamed beasts, subject to his whip and whistle? Not surprisingly, you and your associates regard nicknames as childish and degrading. And yet, in light of your manager's obsession with them, you're somewhat reluctant to do anything about it. Fortunately, if you don't like sharing your name with the inhabitants of your local zoo, there are steps you can take—even if your manager is a bear.

First, you and several of your associates need to meet with him. The set-up is to tell him that you want talk about strategies to improve morale, satisfaction, and productivity. This type of bait is sufficiently tantalizing to tempt most managers, even if they view their employees more as a menagerie than a team.

In this meeting, you'd say something like, "We know the nicknames you've assigned are meant to be playful and fun. We appreciate that, and our concern is that they're getting in the way of business. Other people hear them and use them, and the whole thing ends up being unprofessional and kind of disrespectful, too. It's an interruption and a distraction, and we're convinced that it's hurting our productivity. Is there any chance of getting back to using our actual names?"

This type of query includes several persuasive strategies to convince your manager to nix the nicknames. The first sentence is totally positive and supportive, and so is the first half of the second sentence. Both send a message of appreciation to your manager for making an effort to create a friendly and relaxed atmosphere, and it's impossible for him to disagree with this opener. This also sets the stage for him to be more receptive to whatever follows.

This approach also uses the previously noted technique of substituting "and" for "but," along with keeping the focus away from your manager per se. In this regard, notice that your next point does not focus on your manager's use of these nicknames, but rather focuses on "other people" using them and creating work-related problems. While you clearly indicate that your manager's nicknames are unprofessional and disrespectful, you get the message across without directly slamming him. As a result, he's much more likely to hear the message.

Notice, also, that your final statement is not giving orders to or putting demands on your manager, but simply asking a question that can easily be answered with a yes or no. And further, rather than asking him why he can't use your given names, you're asking if there's "a chance" of using them. Since there's a chance of just about anything, it won't be difficult for your manager to say yes. Unless your manager is as dumb as an ox, as stubborn as a mule, or simply pig-headed, he's likely to show at least some willingness to back away from the barnyard nicknames. Granted, he might not be as quick as a bunny in taking this action, but this should be a good first step in getting this monkey business to end.

As a side note, remember that every time this office idiot utters your nickname and you respond, you're rewarding him. If he continues to animalize your name, you should say your human name back to him in a friendly tone, and then just wait. His next words are likely to be your actual name.

With the passage of a little time, he'll see that there's more to be gained by addressing all of you by your given names—not the names he has given you.

Terms of "Endearment"

Another branch of the office idiot family tree is the colleague or manager who doesn't address employees with nicknames, but uses labels instead. The same principles of power apply, as there's a clear implication that the labeler has more power than the "labelee."

One of the most prevalent forms of this power play is the office idiot who uses pseudo-affectionate terms to address various fellow employees. This includes terms such as "honey," "sweetheart," "beautiful," and "handsome." Rather than intending to show affection, attraction, or romance, these terms are intended to show power, domination, and control. Once again, a person's title or position has no relationship to the propensity to proffer these terms. There are idiotic managers and supervisors who aim them at their subordinates, as well as gaggles of employees who launch them at their co-workers, and minions of employees who even lob them at their boss.

Let's look at a case in which one of your fellow employees has taken to calling you "sweetheart" or "beautiful" or "handsome," and it's making you uncomfortable. You tell him that you don't like these terms, and you even add that they sound like sexual harassment. In true form, the office idiot's response is that these terms are complimentary, so they can't be harassment. The problem is that this power-playing office idiot is woefully, perilously, and even painfully uniformed about the definition of sexual harassment in the workplace. Any unwanted, sexually oriented behaviors fall under the heading of sexual harassment, and that's exactly where his comments lie.

Importantly, even though he thinks "sweetheart," "beautiful," or "hand-some" are compliments, his point of view is meaningless. There's no reason to assume that these terms are perceived positively by whoever is on the receiving end. The only person who gets to determine whether they're compliments, threats, insults, put-downs, or anything else is the recipient.

──────────────────

Since you told this office idiot that you're uncomfortable with these comments and asked him to refrain from making them, the next step is to follow your company's procedure for dealing with claims of sexual harassment, assuming your company has one. If it doesn't, that's an idiotic sign in and of itself. In such a case, you should go to your manager or to your company's HR department and report what you've experienced. There are all sorts of requirements calling for management to promptly investigate such claims and take swift and appropriate corrective action when warranted. At the same time, there's an interesting research finding that may expedite the entire process for you. In a substantial percentage of cases, when sexual harassers are told to stop, they do.

However, telling a harasser to stop means more than saying you don't like what he's saying, and then adding that it "sounds like harassment" to you. Rather, you need to use a strategy that's unequivocal, firm, assertive, and backed up by the threat of real consequences. Having a witness or two doesn't hurt, either. With this in mind, the next time this harasser hits you with an unwanted, sexually oriented label, you'd say, "I've told you before, including on such-and-such date(s), that I find your comments, such as 'sweetheart' and 'beautiful,' to be totally degrading. So-and-so witnessed what you said and is ready to support me if you don't stop. You're upsetting me and ruining this job for me, and this nonsense has to stop right now. If I hear one more of these comments from you, I am going to report this to management, and I'll go outside the company to get help if I need to. Is this clear?"

Sexual harassers are interested in domination and control. If their targets fight back, most harassers will run and hide. It's a power play for them, and when you respond as noted above, harassers see their power slipping away. And typically, that's what they're likely to do, as well.

If this office idiot is still foolish enough to continue addressing you this way, and your company doesn't have the policies or procedures that would make it reasonable for you to try to resolve the matter internally, your next step is to address an employment attorney or the agency in your state that deals with fair employment. Although this office idiot thinks he knows about sexual harassment, he's about to learn a real lesson—the hard way.

11

OFFICE IDIOTS AND THEIR MINDLESS MOTIVATIONAL METHODS

One of the most widely studied topics in the field of management is employee motivation. This research has led to the development and implementation of an extensive array of state-of-the-art tools, tips, processes, and strategies that genuinely enhance motivation on the job. At the same time, these well-founded applications never find their way onto the radar screens of masses of office idiots who either rely on motivational techniques from the Stone Age, or apply motivational methods based on whims, hunches, and anecdotes.

Recognition Ritual

Upon hearing that recognition can be a powerful motivator, some office idiots mindlessly glom onto the idea, totally oblivious to the individual and situational subtleties that determine its impact and effectiveness. For many people, a little knowledge is a dangerous thing—for office idiots, it's the only thing.

For example, let's say your manager has heard that recognition can be a strong motivator, so he wants you to heap more of it onto your reports. Never mind the fact that even mountains of recognition won't amount to a hill of beans if other conditions (such as low pay, harsh working conditions, or miserable benefits) are interfering with employee satisfaction. In his finite wisdom, your manager wants you to pick one day each month for providing your employees with recognition. His goal is to be sure that each of your employees gets recognized at least monthly. The fact that such recognition is mechanical, hollow, and irrelevant has totally escaped him.

After all, recognition that comes like clockwork is meaningless. When there's no link between recognition and behavior, performance, or results, there's no impact on motivation whatsoever. If everyone gets the same recognition at the same time, regardless of what they did, it's little more than background noise. For feedback to have any kind of a lasting impact, it needs to be performance-based and provided as close as possible to the actions that are being reinforced.

So what, exactly, is "recognition"? While it can be a few words of thanks or a congratulatory letter, it can just as easily be a lot more. In fact, there are literally thousands of ways to recognize employees today, running the gamut from advancement to zeppelin rides. As a result, even if monthly recognition worked (which it doesn't), there needs to be clarification and agreement as to what is meant by recognition in the first place.

Another compelling reason to sideline your manager's one-size-fits-all notion is the fact that recognition has a supercharged impact when tailored to the needs and interests of the recipient. This can be as basic as a plant for a high-performing employee who's passionate about gardening, all the way to rewarding employees with credits that they can use online for items they actually want.

This tailoring process prevents the idiotic forms of recognition that end up annoying a recipient, such as the steak dinner that's bestowed on a vegan.

■————————————————————

In dealing with a manager who suggests that you dole out monthly pellets of recognition to your employees, there's no need to get into a disagreement. Rather, tell him, "I think you've raised a very important point, and I want to do even more. Rather than reminding myself to give out recognition on a specific day each month, I'm going to remind myself every day to look for opportunities to provide employees with thanks, credit, recognition, and more whenever they deserve it."

This approach supports your manager's interest in recognition, while making an irresistible offer to him—when you tell people that you're giving them more than they requested, you're markedly increasing the irresistibility of whatever you're proposing. By doing so, you're opening the door to a more effective recognition program.

There's a subtle kicker to this approach, as well. By telling your manager about the important point that he raised, you're actually providing him with some recognition. And that never hurts.

Another Year, Another Yawn

Because opportunities to provide meaningful recognition abound in every workplace, along with the fact that well-conceived and well-timed positive feedback has a compellingly positive impact, there's no reason to stick recognition on the back burner. Unfortunately, this fact easily escapes the purview of garden variety office idiots.

For example, one of the easiest and most logical times to provide employees with some recognition is on the anniversary of their starting date with the company. This date is significant for many reasons, but mostly because employees typically spend more time at work than in any other activity, with the possible exception of sleeping. (Some office idiots manage to combine the two, but that's another matter.) Either way, in light of the chunk of an employee's life that he or she spends at work, a little recognition on his/her anniversary can go a long way on the motivational highway. Unfortunately, when it comes to recognizing employees for their tenure in a company, gaggles of office idiots blithely let these landmarks slide by. So, rather than feeling happy, proud, and energized on their special day, employees feel ignored and even insulted.

For example, let's say that you just passed your third year of employment with a company, but no one in management said a word about it. There's no question that a few words of appreciation would have been nice, but if you go around and fish for recognition, the most likely outcome is that you'll be recognized as needy and dependent. Besides, how meaningful can recognition be if you have to beg for it?

The real problem is that your manager's understanding of recognition and its role in and impact on an organization is buried in the clueless file. The real idiocy is that companies can spend huge amounts of money on employee recognition programs, while your manager just overlooked a freebie that's also one of the easiest recognition points to hit. Remember that recognition is particularly powerful when it's tailored to the individual; what better fits that criterion than the employee's start date? And further, the impact of recognition on this single day increases with each passing year of employment, another fact that typically escapes the community of office idiots.

———————————————

If your manager lets this day slide by without a hint of hype, don't despair—there's actually something you can do to generate that well-deserved recognition while also avoiding the unsavory appellations that can accrue if you appear to be playing the grovel card in your quest for appreciation. All you need to do is write an e-mail to your manager that commemorates your anniversary in a subtle, circuitous manner. For example, you'd write something like, "I noticed that today is my third-year anniversary with the company. I can't believe how fast the years have sailed by, and I just wanted to send you a note saying how much I enjoy working here, especially in terms of the opportunities to learn, grow, and contribute. Thanks very much to you and the management team for these great years."

———————————————

The opening sentence is designed to indicate that you just *happened* to notice that today is your anniversary. The idea behind this phrasing is that it avoids any implication that you might be overly focused on the event. This type of message is virtually guaranteed to generate some healthy recognition in return. Part of what's behind this is the principle of reciprocity: Your e-mail includes kind comments to your manager, and that fact alone is likely to generate a reply that's at least as favorable. Hence, the most likely outcome is that you'll receive your well-deserved recognition.

Constant Reinforcement

Not only are there troupes of idiotic managers who lack even a cursory understanding of motivation, recognition, and the relationship between the two, but there are also packs of non-managerial employees who carry their own hefty baggage into this category. This latter batch of office idiots is typified by their insatiable need for positive reinforcement for everything they do—and even what they don't do. What are the primary motivators for these employees? What do they seek on an ongoing basis? Oh, not much— just constant recognition, attention, credit, accolades, praise, thanks, adoration, approval, adulation, admiration, acknowledgment, and validation. Although many managers try to accommodate these needs, the fact is that this whole matter is trying. Time is wasted whenever these sorts of idiots enter your real or virtual neighborhood, and it's frustrating, stressful, and annoying to feel that you somehow must disburse endless missives of recognition in their direction.

Let's take a situation in which you have one of these office idiots reporting to you. If you don't praise him, he immediately asks you how you think he did, and no matter what you say, he pushes for praise. If he doesn't hear what he wants, he'll praise himself.

■———————————————————

On the one hand, you already understand what it takes to motivate this employee. If you give him projects that provide the opportunity to gain attention and recognition, he'll pursue them diligently in order to meet these needs. The theory behind this type of behavior is that unfilled needs are motivational: Just as a hungry person is motivated to find food, the needy, overly dependent employee will jump into projects if there's any possibility they will feed his need for positive reinforcement.

On the other hand, there's no question that extreme neediness is extremely annoying, and you'll need to talk to him about this. However, what you're seeing is a reflection of deep-seated needs and insecurities that are part of his personality. As a result, there really is no way that a one-on-one conversation is going to suddenly bolster his confidence and self-esteem and instantly eliminate his compelling need for reinforcement.

However, your conversation with him shouldn't focus on his personality, but rather his behavior. Some behaviors can be changed, especially with appropriate feedback and reinforcement. With that in mind, you'd give him some overarching positive feedback on his work, and then let him know that you're very busy and don't always have the time to give him recognition whenever he completes a task. Tell him that your silence in such situations is also saying that he has done a solid job.

And now for the kicker. Say something like this: "I want to do an experiment for the next two weeks. I'll give you intermittent recognition along the way, but it's not going to be ongoing, and I don't want you to seek it. I want you to see that you can continue to do a great job without hearing it all the time from me. You're halfway there already, because you're doing a great job. Do you think you can do this?" If he agrees (and presumably he will, because such experiments are tantalizingly easy to accept), a final step that helps introduce and solidify behavioral change will be for him to write out a statement describing the change, committing to make it happen, and then signing the document. A signed contract with oneself is one of the most powerful ways to introduce real and permanent personal change.

Looking to the future, if you see that he's indeed demonstrating less neediness in his work, you should provide him with positive feedback about that on the spot. This can be as basic as a few words of encouragement to keep up the good work, or something more formalized if you prefer. Either way, this type of feedback will clearly help lock in his new behavior. Ironically, as he demonstrates less of a need for recognition, he's likely to receive more.

The Writing on the Walls

There are legions of office idiots who are perpetually seeking a quick fix to enhance employee motivation. They'd like to grab a hammer and nail, slap something together, and then call it a motivational program. Amazingly enough, some office idiots do this—literally. Their idea of building employee motivation consists solely of nailing some so-called motivational posters onto the walls.

Let's say your company's human resources manager just hung up several of these framed posters around the office. These posters clearly have aesthetic value, with their breathtaking, snow-capped mountain peaks, cascading waterfalls, and uplifting sunrises. And they're also adorned with catchy and somewhat kitschy messages. One such message might be a single word, such as "Strive," while others implore you to reach higher, never give up, go the extra mile, seize your dreams, and similar meaningless missives that you may have also read in yesterday's fortune cookie. While there's nothing inherently wrong with these posters, the fact is that they have far more to do with decoration than motivation.

If your HR manager is truly striving to increase employee motivation, he or she should focus on two key steps. The first is to eliminate key factors that may be interfering with employee motivation, such as inequitable pay, harsh working conditions, inept supervisory practices, or outdated tools and technology. Once these types of dissatisfying elements are corrected, the next step would be to implement practices and programs that provide the employees with opportunities to learn, grow, expand their responsibilities, achieve, attain recognition, and ultimately advance. Attaching pay and other incentives directly to performance has also been found to have a positive impact on employee motivation.

It won't take long for these posters to become little more than wallpaper, literally and figuratively. As such, they'll have as much impact on motivation as the paint on the walls. With that in mind, there's really no need to say or do anything about them. They're visually pleasing, probably quite affordable, and they're not bothering you—so, it's okay if they just hang around.

Hopefully, there's more to your company's motivation program than what meets the eye (that is, the posters).

Selective Recall

When it comes to powerful sources of employee motivation, promotion is often at or near the top of the list. The opportunity for advancement carries with it a combination of some of the strongest work-oriented motivators, including achievement, recognition, responsibility, and more interesting and challenging work. Not surprisingly, office idiots flex their idiocy in every phase of the advancement process. In this regard, one of the most common flashpoints for such idiocy is the tendency to casually lift their employees' hopes about being promoted, only to callously dash them in the eleventh hour.

Let's say your manager tells you that when a position opens up in the future, you'll be promoted. He is totally unequivocal, as is your excitement over this potential career milestone. However, it turns out to be more pretending than portending. When a position opens up that seems to be a perfect match for your skills, experience, and training, it goes to one of your fellow employees instead. As your mental reaction spans a continuum that runs from shock to denial to anger and beyond, you run to your manager. You tell him that the two of you had discussed promotions some months ago, and he said that the next open position would go to you. He gives you a quizzical look and then says, "I said you'd be promoted? I don't remember saying that at all."

At this point, it's game over. You can try to bring him mentally back to the time when he said this, such as by describing where the discussion took place, along with other possibly memorable points in the conversation. However, he isn't likely to have an "Oh, yes!" moment. And, more importantly, the decision has already been made anyway.

■————————————————————

The best you can do at this point is to try to elicit some kind of commitment about a future promotion. Since he apparently made one in the past, perhaps you can choreograph a do-over. With this approach, after you discuss the promotion that went to a coworker, you'd say, "Okay, I understand. Is there a way to put me at the front of the line the next time a position opens up?" Notice that this is a calm and businesslike approach, and you're not threatening or demanding anything; rather, you're simply asking a leading question, and keeping the tone quite informal and friendly. You're certainly not saying that he owes you, even though that's how you feel. This approach uses language that's far more palatable, especially with its soft words about moving to the front of the line. Rather than demanding anything, it's asking a low-key question. If he was willing to make some kind of a commitment about your promotion in the past, this type of query should help open the door for him to do so now.

Like those described in other scenarios in this book, this query also contains a hidden command. Although it would be foolish for you to state, "Put me at the front of the line," that exact directive is actually embedded in your question. If you've established a solid and trusting working relationship with your manager, this message can give him an extra subconscious nudge regarding your candidacy for the next open position. Also, it doesn't hurt to give those eight words a little more emphasis when you say them.

Assuming that your arguably idiotic manager goes along with your request, there's one more step for you to take in this matter, and it's essential. In fact, if you fail to take this step, you're all but guaranteed to have a déjà vu experience all over again when the next opening for a promotion arises. To prevent this outcome, you'll need to send him an e-mail about the discussion, but not just any e-mail: a self-serving e-mail. This type of message doesn't look like a binding document, but it's designed to gently lock your manager into his verbal commitment. It'll also serve as proof of what he said in the event that he has another bout of selective amnesia down the road.

This e-mail would include language such as, "It was great meeting with you today, and I want to thank you for agreeing to put me at the top of the list for the next promotion in our department. I truly appreciate your confidence in me, and I look forward to continuing to advance in our company." In other words, it looks like a thank-you note. It's packaged with highly positive language at the opening and the closing, while the middle clearly reiterates and memorializes the commitment he has made.

———————————————————————————■

At the same time, it's revealing to look a little further at the behavior of this office idiot. It's shocking that he would make any kind of verbal commitment to you about a promotion without following through. Most managers today understand that euphoric and expansive pronouncements to their employees about future employment can be interpreted as contracts, and there's no happy ending for anyone if they are violated. Your manager may indeed claim that he made no such comment to you, but if he keeps this up, he's likely to encounter a different kind of claim—a legal claim.

Rough Ridesharing

Numerous employers today have implemented ridesharing and carpooling programs that are based on proven motivational building blocks. These programs typically include rewards and incentives for employees who not only carpool or vanpool, but also for those who literally take such steps as walking, using public transportation, or riding a bike or motorcycle to work. From the classical motivational standpoint, participants are engaging in positive behaviors, and they're being rewarded for doing so. Such rewards often include companywide recognition, along with drawings, prizes, financial support, special parking, and more. These incentives are augmented by the substantial savings in gasoline costs for the participants.

Employees who participate in these programs not only receive tangible rewards bestowed upon them by their employer, but they also receive a high degree of intrinsic satisfaction by helping to reduce pollution, cut back traffic congestion, save energy, and make a positive contribution to the overall environment. Ridesharing programs sound so easy and seamless that there really should be no way for office idiots to derail them. However, you should never underestimate the ability of office idiots to bring foolishness to even the most foolproof of programs.

Take the case in which your company has a ridesharing program that includes prizes and recognition for the participants. You've been riding to and from work with a couple of your fellow employees, and everything has been working well. Until the other day. You got sick at work, but it was not your day to drive, so your car was sitting in your driveway 30 miles away. As part of the program, your company called a cab for you, but it was very expensive, and—here's the idiotic kicker—you had to pay for it. This provision totally undermines the program and nullifies much of its motivational impact. With this absurd stipulation in place, many would-be participants are likely to become won't-be participants.

In reality, when companies implement ridesharing plans, it isn't uncommon to find a provision that guarantees a free ride home in the event of emergencies, including illness on the job. The idea is to make these plans as easy as possible for the employees to use, and to remove any disincentives that are likely to cause employees to embrace a steering wheel rather than a bus pass.

As noted previously, in order to motivate employees, it's important to first eliminate any factors that may be dissatisfying them. In the case of ridesharing, although your company's program has plenty of motivational trappings, there won't be full participation because the expectation that employees must pay their own way home in the event of illness or an emergency is simply too high a price to pay.

Because you were stuck with a hefty bill due to this flaw in the program, it's appropriate for you to e-mail the program administrator and say the following: "I'm in the rideshare program, and I think it's working really well. Just from talking to the people in my carpool and around the office, I think the one concern is having to pay for a ride home if you get sick or have an emergency. This just happened to me, and now I'm not sure if I can stay in the program. I even heard that there are some employees who are not participating because they don't want to experience what I just went through. I also heard that companies like YYY and ZZZ pay in these situations. I'm wondering if it's worth considering this type of policy as a way to further increase participation. Thanks!"

By opening with a statement indicating that you're in the program, your own credibility is increased far over that of a non-participant. Your opening is further strengthened by an immediate compliment. You're also making inherently undeniable statements that can only be met with agreement, and you've instantly set a positive and palatable tone for whatever follows. Then, by mentioning the practices of other successful companies in your field or industry, it's no longer just your opinion to implement this change, but rather the opinion of other highly influential sources. This element of source credibility instantly increases the likelihood that the recipient will give your suggestion extra credence and consideration. Your message also implies that the recipient will win by going along with your suggestion. After all, he or she will surely get more recognition, credit, and praise if participation in this plan increases—and you're presenting a cost-effective way to make that happen.

The overarching concept is that employees should believe that it pays to carpool. If they need to leave work because of an emergency, then the company pays. Unless the person who's overseeing this plan is so deeply ensconced in office idiocy that he or she can't see the traffic for the cars, you should see some movement on this matter. And, if your manager can read between the lanes and lines, you just might get reimbursed for your cab fare.

12

IDIOTIC BLAMING, DEFLECTING, AND BACKSTABBING

Office idiots don't do many things well, but there's one arena where they have no equal. They're all-stars when it comes to shirking responsibility, blaming others, avoiding work, playing the denial card, and undercutting their fellow employees. They're not prepared for much, but they're always ready to shirk rather than work, fault rather than fix, and create problems rather than solutions.

The Fickle Finger of Blame

Let's look first at the blame game. Let's say your manager has assigned a project to you, but because of his delays in providing you with needed information, you've missed the deadline. Your manager notices the missed deadline, but rather than figuring out what happened, he flips into blame mode and says that you need to "work smarter." Upon hearing this sage advice, you are initially caught off guard, and don't say much in response, especially because you don't have enough facts to make a good case off the top of your head.

Your decision to hold back an initial response to an office idiot in this type of encounter is a good one. When confronted by a blamer who has both fingers pointed at you, the best step is to refrain from an emotional or even a quasi-factual rebuttal, as the Swiss cheese quality of such a reply lends itself to more hole-poking, even by an office idiot. Besides, if he's aware of his own role in the missed deadline, and that's a highly likely supposition, he's already established a denial system that will shield him from whatever you say. And if he's miraculously unaware of his role in the debacle, then nothing you say off the top of your head is going to rouse him from his cluelessness.

Your next step is to look over this entire project from start to finish in order to determine exactly what happened. The objective isn't to find evidence that exonerates you while indicting your manager, but rather to review the situation frame by frame with an eye for better steps that could have been taken at every point along the way. If this approach happens to show that you could not have worked any smarter on this project, then so be it.

With the facts in hand, you're ready to meet with your manager. However, you shouldn't set this up as a meeting where you defend yourself and fillet your manager. Rather, set it up by saying something like, "I think it would be helpful if we met briefly to talk about what happened on this project. I want to team up with you to develop a strategy that prevents this type of outcome in the future." With this approach, you should have no problem getting the meeting. Most people like to help, and by integrating the word "helpful" into your opening sentence, you're instantly yet subtly playing off of this need. Further, your message indicates that you want to talk about what happened, rather than saying that you want to explain yourself or show your manager his mistakes. Importantly, your goal isn't to have him leave the meeting in shambles, but rather for the two of you to team up and jointly develop a strategy to avert missed deadlines in the future.

At no point before, during, or after the meeting is it worthwhile to hit him with the fact that his failure to provide you with information led to the project's demise. Rather, during the meeting, you'd walk through the facts and note the progress that was made at each step, while simultaneously pointing out where some additional data would have been helpful. There's no question as to who should have provided such data and didn't, but there's no reason to rub your manager's nose in it. If you refrain from making comments that would inflame his defensiveness, your ideas are far more likely to be heard. This means that instead of wrapping up the meeting with antagonism, claims, and counterclaims, the outcome will be more communication, coordination, and collaboration, along with a shared understanding of the steps to be taken to prevent a recurrence.

To help solidify this meeting of the minds, you should conclude by saying, "This sounds like a good way to go. I'm going to write a draft of what we just agreed to, and I'll send it to you. Would you mind looking it over, change it as needed, and then get back to me?" Importantly, by using the word "draft," it's clear that you're not forcing anything on your manager. Most people like to tweak a draft, and when your manager includes his own wording, he'll be strengthening his sense of ownership of the document and thereby further binding himself to its terms.

From that point, all that remains is to see what happens on his next outing. Hopefully, it won't be a replay of the idiot and the odyssey.

———————————————————■

The Write-Up Isn't Right

As if it's not bad enough for an employee to be blamed for a failure that's totally due to the idiocy of his or her manager, the topper occurs when a managerial buffoon decides to write up an employee for a failure that belongs in his own lap. And in his own file.

Let's look at a situation in which you're working on a project with your manager, and you're on top of your game. Everything you've been handling is moving along like clockwork. However, as the deadline approaches, it becomes clear that your manager, already known in many circles as an office idiot, drops the ball. Not only does he miss the deadline, but his contributions miss the mark and even miss the point. However, in an act of brazen idiocy, he tosses all of the blame onto you. Rather than making any effort to consider what actually happened, he spews out, "You should have checked in with me! You didn't focus adequately on this project, and you failed to watch the deadlines...." And so on, ad infinitum. Obviously, it's distressing and even depressing to work for a manager for whom the expression "managerial skills" is an oxymoron. Your manager is actually failing in three key areas. First, he's denying accountability for his own mistake; second, he's trying to blame others rather than correct the problem; and third, he's taking disciplinary action against an arguably innocent person.

But carefully notice what else this office idiot is doing. On one level, he's simply illustrating the common practice of projecting one's own shortcomings onto others. At the same time, there's something more sinister at work here— a sneaky and sniveling practice that's particularly popular among idiots who function (or malfunction) in the political arena. He's using a Machiavellian tactic in which he looks at his own inept, incorrect, or inadequate behaviors and then affixes them to his opponents. He can easily convince himself that you're the cause of the failure, while his real goal is to convince everyone else. He figures that if he commits this myth to writing in the form of a disciplinary warning and then gets you to sign it, no further convincing is needed.

As a result, you should tread very carefully here. When you meet with an office idiot who produces a memo that pins this type of failure on you, the first step is to calmly present the facts, just as described in the previous scenario. But be forewarned: when office idiots engage in this type of fiction-writing (the written warning that blames someone else for their misdeeds), they're not particularly receptive to the nonfiction version.

Regardless of the facts you present, he's likely to ask you to sign a write-up that will be placed in your file. You should respond with, "I'm a little confused over what signing the document means. Does it mean that you discussed this matter with me, or does it mean that I agree with its content?" If he indicates that your signature only commemorates the fact that the two of you met about this, then you can sign. After you do so, you'll be given a copy. You'd thank your manager, and then ask, "What's the procedure for writing my thoughts and comments about what happened here? I'd like that in my file, too." Your manager will either tell you how this works, or you'll need to make the same inquiry of your company's HR manager. Notice that your question is free of hostility and aggressiveness, and you're not stating that you want to expose the truth about your manager and what really happened here. All you're asking for is an opportunity to express your thoughts on this matter.

At the same time, if your manager indicates that signing the document means that you agree with its contents, you should refuse to do so. It's 100-percent wrong for you to essentially sign a confession for a crime that you didn't commit. Tell your manager something like, "I think it's unfair for me to sign anything that says I was the cause of the problem. Isn't there a fairer way to handle this?" At that point, stop talking. Notice that with this approach, you're focusing on what is unfair for you, rather than what is unfair about your manager. Also, you're giving your manager some additional time to reflect on the situation. But whatever happens, don't pick up the pen.

If you automatically capitulate and start signing documents that exculpate your manager and implicate you for abysmal outcomes that have nothing to do with your performance, all you're doing is letting your manager know that you're an easy mark who can be stuck with the blame whenever things go wrong. Also, by willingly signing these falsely accusatory memos, you're destined to see more of them down the road. If enough of these stories end up in your file, there won't be a happy ending. However, by demonstrating that you're a person who stands up for your rights and for what's actually right, you're less likely to be called upon to autograph these idiotic fairy tales.

Taking this kind of stance may lead to the involvement of senior management, but that should be just fine with you.

A Matter of Deflection

There's no reason to think that idiotic behaviors such as deflecting, blaming, and backstabbing are limited to the ranks of managers, as there are plenty of rank and file employees who can just as easily engage in these rank behaviors. Even worse, there are surprising numbers of situations in which idiotic managers align themselves with equally idiotic non-managers to jointly insert their swords into the backs of unsuspecting bystanders.

For example, let's say one of your associates goes on a business trip, and your manager e-mails her and asks her to finish up her section of a larger project. You're copied because you're also involved on this project. For whatever reason, your associate doesn't get her work done, and when she returns, she reaches into her bag of idiotic tricks and says that you should have taken care of it since she was on the road. After all, you were copied on the e-mail from your manager. You shake your head in disbelief, but you're confident your manager will review the matter, and when he does, you guardedly hope that he'll set things straight. You know that he has some latent idiotic tendencies, but this situation appears to be idiot proof.

Unfortunately, you overlooked one of the most important truisms in this arena: in the world of office idiots, nothing is idiot-proof. Your manager ends up siding with your coworker and agrees that you should have completed the work while she was on the road. Hence, when it comes to dealing with office idiots, you've got a "two-fer." You get two office idiots for the high price of one.

Let's look a little further at both of the problems in this situation. First, there's your charming coworker. Rather than admitting her mistake, for which there could be any number of plausible explanations, she decides to blame you. She reaches this conclusion in spite of the fact that the work was assigned to her, and no one even hinted that you should do it. In fact, if you had unilaterally completed a project that was assigned to her, you'd come off as controlling, egocentric, and probably more than a little weird.

And then there's your manager. Unless he regards you as clairvoyant, there's no way that his expectation makes any sense. He never asked you to do the work. Rather, your associate simply failed to do her work. If your manager wanted you to step in, all he had to do was say so. Instead, he said nothing—until it was too late.

Your first step is to meet with your manager, express concern over the project's shortfall, and simply tell him the truth: "If I had known that she wasn't able to complete the assignment, I would have gladly helped out." At that point, stop talking and wait for your manager's reply. Since he has already dipped his toe into this pool of idiocy, he's likely to jump all of the way in and say something like, "I expect you to show initiative on the job. I copied you on this e-mail, and I want you to step up in situations like this."

Of course, this type of reasoning is patently idiotic. However, rather than saying anything close to that, you'll get further with,

"I agree with your thoughts about initiative, and I just need to be sure that it's okay with you before I jump in and start doing other people's work. I'm concerned about the difference between taking action and taking over, and I don't want to step on my coworkers' toes and create more problems. However, if you give me the green light, I won't stop until the job's done."

This response provides a reasonable explanation for your actions, while simultaneously setting the stage to correct the problem. All you need is the green light. This approach avoids blaming, name-calling, claims and counter-claims, insults, as well as debates about initiative, excuses, and responsibility. This solution-based strategy will prevent a recurrence of the current turkey, and it'll do so without ruffling your coworkers' feathers.

Of course, a question remains about the coworker who tossed you under the corporate bus. At this point, you know where you stand with her. In the event that you're again copied on an e-mail that's addressed to her and deals with work that she's supposed to complete, you may want to double back and touch base with her and your manager just to see how things are going. Doing so will help you make a preemptive strike, rather than being reactively struck.

Manager of the Blamer

If you turn over a rock at any job level, you're likely to find swarms of blamers, deniers, and backstabbers squirming all over each other, each in an effort to avoid the light of day. Not only are such idiotic creatures likely to be your manager or peer, they can just as easily report to you. After all, today's idiotic managers had to start somewhere—and the art of blaming, denying, and deflecting isn't learned overnight.

Let's say that you're the manager of a burgeoning office idiot whose *modus operandi* is to blame anyone but herself whenever she makes a mistake.

Whether it's a minor slip-up or a major screw-up, she's hard-wired to proclaim her innocence, weave elaborate fabrications and rationalizations, and then implicate anyone who appears to lack plausible deniability. When you approach her about her mistakes on one of your projects, she flips into her defensive demeanor and becomes visibly upset, shaken, hurt, distressed, and angry, all at the same time. Soon enough, she starts implicating and denigrating coworkers, the project itself, departmental standards and expectations, the deadline, the training, the parking, the vending machines, and just about anything else that's upsetting her at the time. All of this is nothing but a giant smokescreen to shield her from the consequences of her poor performance.

Obviously, no one can blame you for being annoyed with an employee who's bent on blaming others. When dealing with this type of office idiot, there are a few key strategies to consider.

━━━━━━━━━━━━━━━━━━━━━━━━

The first is best described as preventive management. The idea is to stop this employee from making masses of mistakes before she even starts. This means that you'll need to ramp up the amount of guidance, coaching, feedback, and follow-up that you give her. If you see her heading down the wrong path, you'll be there to put on the brakes, redirect her, and give her targeted, hands-on training as needed. Importantly, you shouldn't make these interventions regularly scheduled events, lest she come to expect them and possibly set the stage to make things look better than they really are. Rather, you should have a few formal feedback sessions, hyphenated by briefer, impromptu discussions where you look carefully at what she's doing, how she's doing, and where immediate course corrections are needed.

This approach isn't based on frequent perfunctory communications, such as, "Is everything going okay?" Such a leading question is destined to receive an affirmative response, even if she has just steered the ship into an iceberg. Rather, the idea is to spend a few minutes with her and drill deeply into her work. Your comments would include something like, "I just wanted to stop by, see how things are going, and see if I can help you with anything. Where are you with the such-and-such part of this assignment?" After she pulls this up on her monitor, you can continue with your line of questions, but continue to avoid questions that call for a yes-or-no response. Questions such as "Is it going okay?" or "Do you have what you need?" or "Will it be done on time?" are all going to get a yes, and there's no reason to assume that this is an accurate reply.

As noted previously, if you really want to get some useful information, there are open-ended questions that can easily be substituted for the most common types of leading questions. For example, instead of asking, "Is the project going okay?" you'd say, "Tell me how the project is going." Instead of, "Do you have what you need?" you'd say, "What else do you need?" And rather than asking, "Will it be done on time?" you'll get a more meaningful response by asking, "When do you think you'll be done?"

Finally, be sure that the feedback you provide is focused on her errors rather than on her. If she senses that she's being personally attacked, she's likely to try to defend herself, and not surprisingly, you'll see more defensiveness. By using more of a teaching and coaching approach that focuses on her work, output, and results, you'll find her to be less defensive—and less offensive, too. And if you see her making improvements and fewer errors, be sure to include some positive reinforcement during your visits.

Looking further down the road, if you find that this employee is still mired in errors and finger-pointing, all in spite of your efforts to rescue her from the grips of office idiocy, one final suggestion comes to mind. Perhaps the real error is for her to continue in this line of work. And if this is the ultimate outcome, she'll ironically have no one to blame but herself.

———————————————————■

Virtually Backstabbed

Office idiots who are inclined to engage in blaming, backstabbing, and deflecting often find that e-mail is an ideal medium for transmitting their underhanded messages. Their words travel at the speed of light, and there's a real advantage to being the first message on the block. By launching a first strike that undercuts a coworker, the backstabbing office idiot instantly forces his or her target to come up with an explanation for whatever is claimed. And when the accused starts presenting his or her side of the story, especially without adequate preparation, it's easy to overexplain and thereby look weak and guilty.

For example, let's look at a situation in which you're on a committee composed of employees from several different departments. Part of your role is to work with one committee member to develop a new feature that will be accessible to all employees through your company's home page. While you work diligently on this project, your so-called colleague does practically nothing, but he's always ready to criticize. When you run a beta test of the program, he notices a minor bug, but rather than saying anything directly to you, he sends a critical e-mail to your manager and to everyone else on the committee. As a preemptive strike, this bombshell makes you look bad, while making the idiotic backstabber look good. And therein lies his motive.

Your initial instinct is to respond with a firm, forceful, thorough e-mail to him and everyone else that spells out what *really* happened. Such a response would provide details on the various tests while also describing the strategies to debug the program. Unfortunately, most of the committee members are not going to take the time to read your summary, especially if it looks long, clunky, and cumbersome. Besides, they don't want to get into the middle of a virtual battle. And those who do read your e-mail won't know whom to believe, especially if your backstabbing associate writes a rebuttal. By continuously muddying the waters, he can bring more chaos, confusion, and debate to this debacle, all of which further weaken your stance.

The best step for you to take is go face-to-face with this office idiot, as well as with the members of the committee and your own manager. Prior to any such close encounters, you should put together a brief and clear statement regarding the bug and the debugging. You should review it, tighten it, and even practice saying it to the point that the wording is totally natural and comfortable. This is what you'll be saying to your manager and to the committee at large.

However, your comments to the backstabber will be a little different, and he should be your first stop. In fact, if you don't approach him right out of the gate, one of the first things your manager will ask is whether you've discussed the matter with him. By hitting the backstabber first—not literally, of course—you'll be ready with a yes to that question, rather than letting it derail your discussion before it even leaves the station.

When you go face-to-face with the backstabber, it would be a mistake to open with an attack on his underhanded and self-serving e-mail. As annoying as his antics have been, such an overture will only enflame the situation, generate more animosity, and encourage further untoward behaviors. A more productive approach would be to say something like, "I'm glad you found that bug. I've got some ideas about fixing it, and I wanted to talk to you about them." At that point, mention the strategies that you have in mind and give him a bona fide opportunity to present his input. Without his participation, he's going to criticize whatever you do. However, if his ideas are incorporated in the fix, he's not likely to be critical, lest he criticize himself.

Before wrapping up the meeting, there's one more point to make, and it goes like this, "In the future, if you find problems, glitches, or bugs, we both can save a lot of time and do a better job if you let me know, rather than instantly e-mailing everyone. Can we agree to give this a try?" With this approach, you've clarified what's in it for him if he gives your suggestion a try, especially in terms of saved time and improved quality. After all, one key way to induce someone to change a behavior is to show how he or she will benefit from the change. Remember that the other person is thinking, *What's in it for me?* By outlining the benefits and advantages associated with the changed behavior, that question is answered. Another less apparent, yet equally persuasive element of this approach is the team-oriented context that's established by frequent use of the word "we." And by once again using the strategy of giving something "a try," rather than going for a permanent change, you're making it much easier for your backstabbing associate to go along with what you're suggesting.

When you meet with your managers and the committee, don't even bring up the conniving e-mail. Rather, let them know that there was indeed a bug in the system, and then briefly mention the cause of the problem, the steps you'll be taking to fix it, and the final date when the new feature will be good to go. If your managers and fellow committee members have anything on the ball, they'll recognize your associate's behavior for exactly what it is. Self-aggrandizement. Self-promotion. Backstabbing. And by refraining from stooping to his level to deal with it, you'll be sending a clear message about him, along with a clearer and better message about you.

Frying Former Employees

Office idiots who thrive on backstabbing and blaming can find no greater pleasure than casting aspersions on people who are incapable of defending themselves. Such hapless victims appear to have no choice but to absorb these untruths while the office idiots emerge absolved and unscathed. The process is simple enough. The office idiots amass all of their own crises, failures, and debacles, do a little rephrasing, repackaging, and sidestepping, and then—poof! The office idiot's slate is wiped clean, and all of his or her failures are now fully owned by someone else.

Who would sit back silently in the face of such a one-sided transfer? No one—other than former employees who are no longer around to set the record straight. When employees leave a company, regardless of the reason, office idiots start salivating over the opportunity to take everything that has gone wrong and dump it on their less-than-dearly departed coworkers. Of course, the fact that this blame-switch is unfair, unwarranted, unprofessional, and unkind means nothing to an office idiot. Rather, such departures are viewed as a chance to hit their own restart button. There may be other employees who not only regard this practice as wrong, but also see it as counter-productive, demoralizing, and disgusting. But when office idiots hear this pushback, they simply await the day for these "hypocrites" to leave the company so that to-day's crises can be dumped on them.

Let's say you work for a company where such lopsided finger-pointing pre-vails. Whenever employees leave, whether on their own or because they were terminated, various office idiots say terrible things about them and their work, and attribute the bulk of the company's current problems to them. The truth, however, is that some of the former employees actually did a good job while working for the company, and you and several of your fellow employees are getting pretty tired of this practice of endlessly blaming them for everything that has gone wrong.

In reality, when current employees go out of their way to make disparag-ing remarks about former employees, it's actually the current employees who look bad. Their blame-smearing comments reek of pettiness, vindictiveness, and unfairness. And further, while office idiots who make such comments think they have a new beginning, the only thing that's really beginning is an increase in coworker wrath and disgust. After all, you and your associates most likely know the real causes behind the problems that your company is facing today. While some may indeed be the result of a former employee or two, today's complex organizational issues rarely go back to the actions of any single former employee. In fact, if you really want to see the sources of such problems, look carefully at the employees who are so quick to cast the blame upon others—especially upon those who are unable to utter a word in their own defense.

Your objective is not to somehow restrict freedom of speech, but this situation definitely warrants discussion with senior management—assuming that they are not part of the blaming brigade, too. Rather than trying to handle this matter on a solo basis, you and a few of your associates should have a sit-down discussion with a member of the senior management team and let him or her know what's going on.

You'd set up such a meeting by indicating that you'd like to discuss a situation that's interfering with employee morale, motivation, performance, productivity, and loyalty. Since these are all emotionally charged words for any member of management, most managers at this level would be interested in hearing whatever you and your associates have to say.

In presenting your thoughts on this matter, you should be direct and honest, such as by saying, "We know that some employees who left the company arc responsible for various problems that we're facing today, but we're concerned about a couple of related issues. First, former employees are constantly being blamed for today's problems, and that's not fair. Some of them really did a great job for us. And second, we think it makes sense to change the dialogue at some point, stop blaming previous employees for today's problems, and just hunker down and get to work on solving them. At some point, the problems are ours and not theirs, and we think that point is now, and we're ready to jump in and do whatever is needed."

The structure of these comments is similar to a motivational speech in which you set the foundation and then start building momentum that leads to a powerful winning crescendo and conclusion. Your comments open with a string of undeniably true statements, while avoiding name-calling, whining, and complaining. In the place of such distractions are more emotionally charged words that have special meaning for many managers and leaders, such as "hunker down," "get to work," and a readiness to "jump in." This is a problem-solving approach that concludes with a call to action. When you use an intentionally vague expression indicating that you'll "do whatever is needed," managers who hear these words will unconsciously fill in the specifics required to get the job done, and then sense that your suggestions are in sync with theirs.

As a side note, individuals who launch insults at former employees should wake up and realize that an equally derogatory verbal assault just might await their departure from the company. And many remaining employees are likely to believe that such an assault would not be wholly inaccurate or unwarranted.

13

OFFICE IDIOTS IN TRAINING

For office idiots, training programs are showplaces where they can model their idiocy in a wide variety of roles and capacities. For example, there are idiotic outside trainers whose expertise is apparently limited to charging outrageous fees, managers and supervisors whose training practices are a study in absurdity, fellow employees who'd enhance any training program by being in absentia, and mentors whose understanding of training is best measured in nanograms (a nanogram being one billionth of a gram).

Employee training and development programs and practices have the potential to enhance a company's effectiveness, add to the value of every participating employee, and make a measurably positive impact on individual and companywide motivation, productivity, and performance. However, when such programs suffer from an infestation of office idiocy, training is draining in every respect.

The Amateur Training Professional

On the one hand, there are some outstanding trainers whose expertise, understanding of the learning process, and didactic skills all come together to forge a first-rate educational experience for all employees who are fortunate enough to attend their programs. At the same time, there are gaggles of would-be trainers whose practices, presentations, and programs are studies in futility rather than utility.

Let's look at a situation where your company has dipped into that latter grab bag and pulled out a trainer who presents himself as an expert on preventing sexual harassment on the job. Such training is regarded as important in your workplace, and your company also falls under a state law that mandates such training for all supervisory personnel.

Along with several fellow managers, you just sat through a sexual harassment prevention seminar presented by this outside "expert." Unfortunately, at the conclusion of the seminar, all that you and most of your fellow attendees could conclude is that the session was a waste of time and money. You're particularly annoyed with the trainer's frequent use of questionable sexual language and jokes. He even touched and verbally harassed several attendees, all in an inglorious attempt to illustrate various inappropriate, sexually oriented behaviors.

When employees emerge from sexual harassment prevention training and feel more violated than educated, it's apparent that something has gone horribly wrong. And that something is the trainer. Although effective training practices call for a variety of teaching strategies to accommodate the attendees' different learning styles, the idea is to use a mixture of techniques that include discussions, questions and answers, case studies, role playing, practice, and feedback. Notice that such techniques as abusing, insulting, degrading, grabbing, groping, and harassing are not on the list.

———————————————————————————

At this point, your best step is to meet with whoever retained the idiotic trainer and his program for your company. Prior to such a meeting, you and some of your fellow managers should put together a summary of this trainer's outrageous antics, backed up with verbatim examples of his language plus clear descriptions of what he did. The objective of such a meeting is to inform management of the unacceptable nature of the trainer's actions, the consequences associated with having an idiot in this role, and the steps that should be taken from this point. Early in the discussion, you should be sure to say something like, "We think it's a great idea to provide training on sexual harassment prevention. The problem is that we just sat through a very questionable seminar, and the bottom line is that we vote for pulling the plug on it right now."

With this wording, you're emphasizing your support for the program, which also implies support for the manager you're addressing. In addition, by indicating that you just sat through the seminar, your credibility is increased because you were in the line of fire, rather than simply talking about issues that you heard from someone else. Notice that you're not only using fairly informal wording to suggest that this debacle needs to end immediately, but you're also using more visual language. Consider the difference between the following two recommendations regarding this program: "We strongly recommend that management end it immediately" vs. "We vote for pulling the plug on it right now." It's clear that the latter phrasing is more visual and memorable, and therefore much more impactful.

With this framework in place, you'd then briefly yet factually describe some of the more heinous behaviors displayed by the trainer during the session. Your tone should be calm and businesslike, and you should pay careful attention to the manager's responses and body language to be sure that your points are hitting home. When you sense that your messages have landed, it's time to ask a closing question, such as, "What do you think?" At this point, the manager should have no difficulty in reaching for the plug and pulling it. Unless the trainer is this manager's brother-in-law or has some other surreptitious connection to the company, he should definitely wind up in the "one and done" category.

It's totally unacceptable to have a sexual harassment prevention program that shows the attendees how to harass, treats such behaviors so lightly as to practically condone them, and then ends up creating a sexual harassment incident (a hostile environment) in and of itself.

Missing the Point with Bullet Points

One popular training technique is the use of a PowerPoint presentation that's composed primarily of bullet points. Typically, the trainer shows a slide with one brief point, discusses it with the group, and then clicks for the next point to appear. This approach takes advantage of several factors that help increase learning, such as two-way communication, opportunities to practice with the material that's presented, repetition, presentation of information in small chunks, and feedback. Naturally, all of this falls by the wayside when the bullet points are developed and then presented by an office idiot.

For example, take the scenario in which your manager informs you and several of your associates that she wants to provide an update on some key developments in your field. Shortly thereafter, she sets up a training session for all of you. Unfortunately, your manager's idea of training is to flash extraordinarily lengthy bullet points on the screen, and then read each point to you, word by word, line by line—for *two hours*. As part of this snooze fest, she prefers that all attendees hold their questions until the end. Of course, when that hallowed moment finally arrives, there's only one question on everyone's mind: "Are we done yet?"

Perhaps the biggest problem with this idiotic approach to training is that flashing a bunch of bullet points on a screen and then reading them to the attendees really isn't training. Where's the interaction, the variety in presentation techniques, the feedback? In fact, where's the learning? And by the way, research continues to find that one of the least effective training methods is a lecture. And further, it's amazing how many office idiots continue to believe that bullet points in training should be lengthy sentences or paragraphs, as long as they're preceded by a black dot. In actuality, bullet points work best to briefly highlight the central topics, issues, data, questions, or summaries. They don't work so well as dissertations.

When a training session is little more than a two-hour reading activity for the trainer, there's no need for the session at all. Rather, the entire presentation should be e-mailed to the attendees, and they can read it themselves.

■────────────────────────

Because your manager's idea of training is wedded to reading interminable bullet points to hapless attendees, your only shot at salvaging any of this is to meet with her and see if you can shed some light on her (ironically) pointless approach to bullet points. With this in mind, a few of you would meet with her shortly after one of her sessions. The idea is to follow one of the most widely accepted principles of learning—that is, providing feedback as closely as possible to the behavior in question (or, in this case, to the questionable behavior). Let her know that you and some of your associates would like to meet with her to talk about making the best use of the training that she's providing. As she's apparently devoted to what she thinks is training, you shouldn't have much difficulty setting up such a meeting.

During the meeting itself, you'd open by saying, "We know you're doing a huge amount of work summarizing the main training points and presenting them during your training sessions." Once again, you're using a statement that can only generate agreement, while subtly opening the door to your forthcoming comments. You'd then focus on the ways that her program could be even better, such as by saying, "There's so much we can learn from your programs, but with all of the time it takes to go through the bullet points, we can't ask the questions or have the discussions that would help us really learn and apply the new information to our jobs." With this approach, you're not criticizing your manager or her knowledge base. In fact, you're complimenting her and showing interest in learning more from her and thereby strengthening your ability to do your work.

She may proffer a suggestion or two, such as by mentioning that perhaps she could conduct longer sessions—heaven forbid! You should give cursory consideration to such a suggestion, and then kindly put the kibosh on it by offering a suggestion of your own by saying, "That's an interesting idea, and we think we could learn even more if you sent your bullet points to us before the meeting and let us read through them. Then, at the meeting, we'd be able to discuss them, learn a lot more about them, and determine how to best apply them to the job. This would save you time, increase our learning, and improve our work. Do you think we can try something like this at our next meeting?"

———————————————————————————■

This approach has all sorts of wins for your manager, such as better use of her time, increased learning for her employees, application of her points to the job at hand, and, ultimately, improved performance. Further, your closing question isn't asking for the world. You're not asking your manager to make anything close to a major change or commitment; you're simply asking her to give your approach a try during the next meeting.

The wording of the closing question also keeps the door open for your manager to include some of her own thoughts, all as a result of the insertion of two words: "something like." Look at the difference in tone and meaning between the following two closing sentences: First, the suggested closing sentence, "Do you think we can try something like this at our next meeting?" Now look at the exact same sentence without those two words, "Do you think we can try this at our next meeting?" It's clear that the first question is more outreaching, inclusive, and collaborative—and, ultimately, more acceptable.

Hopefully, this experience will help your manager learn about bullet points, while helping you and your colleagues earn a few points of your own.

Keep the Change

One of the most effective ways for managers to introduce and implement change is to approach the process from the standpoint of training and coaching. After all, change implies learning, whether it's in terms of new assignments, expectations, policies, procedures, standards, schedules, layouts, plans, or objectives. Unfortunately, this fact escapes the herds of office idiots who literally fall under the title of manager. For them, the concept of introducing change is quite simple: They dump it onto their employees and advise them to just go with it. Forget about the fact that the employees have no understanding of the change or its rationale, will most likely stick to their old ways of doing things, and will be even more resistant the next time the winds of change blow.

Let's look at a case in which your manager's idea of change management is restricted to sorting nickels and dimes in his pocket. When he introduces any kind of change in your department, such as the implementation of new practices or procedures, all he does is stand in front of you and your associates and spew them out. If any of you raise a question or voice a concern, his immediate reaction is that you're "resistant to change." And then, in a blaze of unmitigated office idiocy, he says that he understands your pushback because it's human nature to resist change. He says that you'll get used to his changes in time.

━━━━━━━━━━━━━━━

The reality is that when it comes to introducing change, your manager needs to change his ways. And that means that you and some of your cohorts need to have a sit-down with him. You'd start the process by saying, "We'd like to meet with you so we can be sure to implement your changes correctly." The beauty of this upbeat and positive approach is its unspoken message, "If we don't meet, there's no way to fully and correctly implement your changes. So, unless you want your changes to go down the drain, you better sit down with us."

At the outset of such a meeting, the objective is to show your manager the specific changes that are confusing you. The idea is to walk through every change until you feel that you can run with them. At the same time, although your purported goal is to clarify the changes that he piled on all of you, the larger goal is to see if you can open his eyes to a better way to introduce change per se. With that in mind, you should bring up his favorite topic—human nature and resistance to change. Although you're not going to be conducting a philosophy class for your manager, there's a learning point that may jolt his thinking.

To get the ball rolling, you'd say something like, "We also want to talk to you about resistance to change. You said it's human nature." He'll almost definitely respond in the affirmative, which opens the door for your next comment: "Okay, let's say we're going to introduce a change in your life that will dramatically alter your job, where you live, and your relationship with your family and friends. Sounds like a pretty big change, doesn't it?" Once again, he'll agree. At that point, you say, "Okay, you just won the lottery, and you'll be pocketing a cool $65 million. Presumably, this is a big change. Are you going to resist it?" This time, of course, he'll say no. And when he does, you respond with, "But you said it's human nature to resist change. What's really going on?" You then cut right to the chase and say, "People don't automatically resist change. Rather, they resist its unknown aspects. What's the change? Why is it being made? How is it going to affect me? By letting people know more about a change and its impact on the players, their resistance immediately drops. What do you think?"

After he expresses his thoughts, say, "And there's even more!" This type of phrase will break the cadence of any discussion. As a result, it'll grab your manager's attention and heighten his interest in whatever you're about to say. As a quick aside, other phrases that also have this power include "And that's not all," "And one more point," and "By the way." Now that you've hooked his attention, your next words would be, "You know, if we had an opportunity to learn about some of the changes you have on the drawing board, we could probably add some pretty good ideas. And as far as resistance to these changes, there'd probably be none. It's pretty tough to resist our own ideas."

As your manager responds, you'll see if his idiotic conceptions have been shaken at all, or whether they're simply frozen in times gone by. If you do see the slightest twinge of receptiveness to a more interactive approach to implementing change, you'd wrap things up by saying, "I know this sounds corny, but if we can be part of the process, we guarantee that these changes will work better." This isn't an offer that he can't refuse, but it's pretty close.

And by the way, the word "guarantee" is one of the most powerful terms in the entire persuasive process. With a guarantee, your manager is more likely to realize that by going along with you, he has nothing to lose—other than a little idiocy.

A Disruptive Force

Idiocy in training often emanates from the ineptitude and inadequacy of whoever is doing the training, but not always. Sometimes the role of the idiot is played by one of the learners (to use that term quite loosely). These idiotic attendees are capable of demonstrating any number of inappropriate and unwanted behaviors, such as by being braggarts, know-it-alls, interrogators, jokesters, texting junkies, sleepers, hecklers, pests, or all-around brats. Given the slightest opportunity, these office idiots can turn any training program into a train wreck.

Let's assume that you're a manager, and your company periodically retains outside trainers to conduct sessions on current management topics. Your manager has selected you and several other managers from her team to attend. The presenters are uniformly excellent, and you've found that these sessions add value and strengthen your leadership and managerial skills. Unfortunately, your sessions are also "blessed" with the presence of a notorious office idiot who has no qualms about interrupting the trainers and everyone else, contradicting what the trainers are saying, arguing with anyone who disagrees with him, blabbing about his own expertise, and constantly rolling his eyes.

Because this idiot in training is ruining the educational experience for everyone, the question is what to do about him. It's nothing more than wishful thinking to hope that as long as the company is providing management education, perhaps such topics as interpersonal communication, group dynamics, and dealing with difficult people will send a message to him. The regrettable reality is that he's intent on sending his own message to everyone else.

■―――――――――――――

Right off the top, there are two key actions to take if you want to have a shot at getting this runaway trainee back on track. The first is to spend some face-time with the disruptive employee himself. However, you shouldn't face him alone, but rather with a posse of two or three fellow managers who also attend these training sessions.

In this meeting, you would use an assertive strategy that may have even been covered in one of your previous management training sessions. In opening it, you'd say, "We know you have management experience and expertise, and some of your comments in these sessions are good. At the same time, excessively contradicting the trainers isn't helping the learning experience for anyone. For example, in the last session on such-and-such a date, there were at least [number] of these interruptions, followed by arguing with the trainer and with four of us. We don't want to squelch debate, but fighting and forcing views on others is a different matter. So, here's the question: Can this be toned down or do we need to get management involved?" After you ask this question, stop talking. Notice the forced-choice aspect of your final question. Given a choice, your disruptive colleague is far more likely to opt for toning things down rather than getting management involved.

If he commits to setting his disruptive behaviors aside, wrap up the meeting and wait to see how he behaves at the next outing. If, by some miracle, he gets with the program rather than destroys it, the three of you should voice some words of thanks and appreciation to reinforce his new behavior. However, if he continues his troublemaking behaviors at the next outing, you and the posse will need to pay a visit to your manager and spell out exactly what has been going on.

You'd approach your manager by saying that you want to talk about a problem that's interfering with the training program. And when you meet, you'd say, "We're enjoying the program, and we think the trainers are first rate. At the same time, there's a problem that's undercutting all of the sessions, and we don't know what to do about it. It's [employee's name]." At this point, stop talking and let your manager process this. Her most likely response will be something like, "What's going on?" You'd then provide a brief and behaviorally based reply, such as, "Well, he's always arguing with the trainers and the rest of us, interrupting the trainers throughout their presentations, and constantly pushing his point of view on everyone. We've spoken with him and gotten nowhere. We're not happy about coming to you, but we know there's a lot to be gained from this training, but he's preventing it from happening." Once you've said this, stop talking. More than likely, your manager will respond by saying that she'll talk with him. You can certainly agree with this strategy, as such a discussion just might put an end to his commitment to confrontation.

As a side note, you may want to pose one more question, "Do you think it would be useful if you were to attend a training session or two? That would definitely tone him down." This approach is actually an indirect way for your manager to deal with this matter. Your manager would not need to say anything to him, as her mere presence at the sessions would do the talking. At the same time, your disruptive fellow manager would transition to docile mode for as long as your manager attends. Beneath the surface of this approach, a key component of behavioral change comes into play. While changes in attitudes can change behavior, changes in behavior can change attitudes. Hopefully, as this resident idiot experiences what it means to act like an adult in a training session, he may come to realize that there are some pretty good outcomes associated with doing so.

Shortcut vs. Undercut

Now that we've covered the training provided by managers and outside consultants, let's look at some other people who play a key role in the training process, namely, the rank-and-file employees who train their peers. In some instances, these employees are given formal training responsibilities, and they may even carry the additional title of mentor. At the same time, there are burgeoning ranks of employees who provide training and guidance to their peers on an informal or casual basis, often without the sanction, knowledge, or approval of management. In this latter confederacy of coworkers, it's not difficult to find some who have been with a company for a good stretch of time and amassed a storehouse of knowledge that can be very helpful to their peers, especially the newbies.

However, unrestrained training isn't without its issues and idiocy. For example, many people who provide this training, often in the form of guidance, suggestions, and advice, are not trained in the process of educating and developing others. This opens the door to an entire universe of educational errors, such as imparting too much or too little information at once, assuming that recipients have successfully absorbed the imparted information (when nothing could be further from the truth), and using training methodologies that are a total mismatch for the learning style of the would-be trainee.

For example, some people are auditory learners who thrive when exposed to training that includes a good deal of discussion. Handing a bursting binder to such a person is one of the least effective ways to impart information to him or her, but that blip doesn't hit the radar screens of many informal trainers. Also, when training is informally imparted from one employee to another, it's often disjointed and helter-skelter, primarily because it's provided while the teacher and learner are simultaneously carrying out their actual job duties. Importantly, work-related demands instantly trump the training process, often leaving the trainee with an incomplete understanding of whatever is being taught.

Oftentimes this knowledge transfer is nothing more than employees passing their own bad habits along to their peers. And when training is provided in a casual and unmonitored framework, erroneous practices can be passed off as acceptable. For example, let's say that you recently joined a company and went through a review of your responsibilities with your manager. As soon as you start applying what you were taught, several of your coworkers say you're doing your work the "long way," and then show you their shortcuts. Their way is indeed faster, but you're not sure about following your peers instead of following your manager. As you consider your coworkers' advice, you come to the conclusion that it's idiotic. Perhaps it's a little faster and easier, but the quality of work is inferior, and a few seemingly important steps are being sidestepped.

———————————————————

Your first move in such a situation is to discuss your coworkers' suggested strategies for getting the job done in more detail. The idea isn't to prove that you're smarter, more dedicated, or more serious about the job. In fact, the idea isn't to prove anything. You're simply interested in learning more about the rationale behind your coworkers' suggestions, as well as their thoughts about what you see as shortcomings in the shortcuts.

Your comments to them might go something like this: "I really appreciate your ideas on how to do the job quicker, and I've got a couple of questions. Is it just me, or is this approach sacrificing quality? And if I'm not incorporating your suggestions correctly, can you check out how I'm doing the work and show me what else needs to be tweaked?" Notice that you're using a Socratic approach that's heavily based on asking questions. Importantly, your questions aren't put-downs or condescending queries. You're not implying any criticism of your fellow employees, nor are you trying to tell them how to do the job. Rather, your approach is a respectful and even somewhat self-deprecating presentation in which you're simply expressing interest in continuing the learning process so that you can fully and correctly apply their suggestions.

On the one hand, as you learn more from your peers, you might find that their suggestions make more sense than you initially thought. If so, you may want to reconsider. Unfortunately, the more likely outcome is that you'll find that with further explanations, their suggestions are actually worse than idiotic. If that's the case, you should continue to do your work in accordance with the guidance you received from your manager. There's no need to pursue the matter any further with your associates, as they're fully wedded to their quicker and easier way to get the job done, and they're not likely to be receptive to comments or suggestions that might rock their comfy boat.

However, you have a decision to make, and it's based entirely on the nature of the shortcuts. Are they fairly harmless or are they creating potentially significant problems? For example, if the shortcuts are undercutting safety, warranties, standards, or end-user expectations, then it's time to have a chat with your manager. Of course, the one thing that is immediately called into question is his competence. After all, if he were on top of his game, he'd already know that his employees are failing to follow the established protocols in carrying out their work. It's no secret that today's most effective leaders manage by wandering around and, as a result, have a pretty clear idea of what their employees are doing. Rather than wandering around, it's quite possible that you're dealing with a managerial idiot who's wondering around.

Nonetheless, if you've determined that these shortcuts warrant a meeting with him, your comments should be blame free, constructive, and team oriented. For example, you'd say something like, "I'm concerned about a situation in our department, and maybe you're aware of it, or perhaps I'm missing something. In fact, I could be totally wrong. I don't want to create a problem with the rest of the team, so can we talk about something confidentially?" Notice that with this approach, you're coming in with questions, not answers, accusations, or arrogance. In this way, you're making it easier for your manager to discuss the situation with you, and to do so without sensing that he's being attacked or insulted. In fact, you're being respectful by indicating that he might already know about the problem, as well as by concluding with an open-ended question that includes a disarming statement in which you say that you might be wrong on this entire matter.

Notice also your low-key request for confidentiality. Nothing is going to be gained if your manager takes whatever you say and then approaches your coworkers and basically says that you're complaining about the way they're doing their jobs. And further, your request for confidentiality further underscores the seriousness that you attach to this matter.

With these opening remarks in place, your next step is to go through the shortcuts, line by line. And from the training standpoint, it's ironic that your manager's subsequent comments and actions are likely to be one of your more compelling learning experiences.

Was It Worthwhile or Worthless?

With all of the training in today's workplaces, one critical question is typically missed by masses of misguided office idiots—namely, is the training doing any good? Without an intelligible answer to this question, a training program is destined to be a draining program—a drain on the employees' time and the company's money. At the same time, in numerous instances where evaluations are indeed conducted, the techniques and methods are strictly dinosaurian.

Let's look at a situation in which you're a manager, and your company has retained an outside consultant to conduct a management training program. You sit through all 12 sessions, including the final meeting. By and large, you think the training is pretty good. As promised, the program includes an evaluative component that consists of a questionnaire for all of the participants. You and the other attendees are asked to rate, on a five-point scale, the trainer, the presentations, how much you enjoyed the sessions, how much you learned, and how much of the training will actually apply to your job. The average score comes out slightly above four, so senior management is seriously considering implementing this training on a companywide basis. At a first glance, this sounds ideal. At a second glance, it sounds idiotic.

■————————————————

Fortunately, you and some of the other attendees have been invited to present your thoughts on this next step. As you do so, there are obviously some positive points to mention, along with that second glance at the evaluation process. With this in mind, you would say, "We attended the management education program, and most of the sessions were really good. We heard that the evaluations averaged over four on a five point scale, and we wanted to talk a little bit about that, if that's okay with you."

Once you get the green light, you'd say, "The four-plus rating is basically a measurement of our reaction. It means that we liked the training and the trainer, but it doesn't say anything about what we learned or how it actually impacted the way we do our jobs. We're not sure it's worthwhile to commit to this training based solely on a reaction. What do you think?"

When the discussion on this point concludes, you'd continue, "The evaluation also asked us to assess how much we learned, but if you really want to see what we learned, we should be given a test. I'm not necessarily suggesting that, but that's how you measure learning. And further, even if we do well on a test, it doesn't mean we're applying our new knowledge to the job. Maybe the new knowledge doesn't even apply at all. So, we think there's probably more to this process than acquiring information. Do you agree?"

When the discussion wraps up, you'd say, "Here's the bottom line. If we're really going to evaluate the effectiveness of this training program or any other, we should take a look at where training is really needed, establish clear performance measurements before the training, set measurable goals for improvement, and then look at the difference in performance before the training versus after. How does this sound to you?" Ironically, you're actually training your managers on the process of evaluating a training program. You'll soon see what they learned.

———————————————————————————————■

Training is an expensive proposition. As of this writing, it's estimated that companies across the United States spend more than $150 billion per year training their employees. When companies make this type of investment in other business areas, there's no question that serious evaluations follow. Such evaluations are clearly composed of more than the participants' reactions.

After all, anything less than a thorough, analytical, and quantitative evaluation would be, well, idiotic.

14

OUTRAGEOUS BEHAVIORS, EVEN FOR OFFICE IDIOTS

While many idiotic behaviors fall into categories, such as the rampant idiocy that pervades the pre-employment process, e-mail, or training, there are some stand-alone displays of idiocy that are so far off the chart that they enter an even higher stratum—namely, the zone of hyper-idiocy.

These antics form a potpourri of idiocy in its most unique and egregious forms. Let's take a look at what's cooking in this pot...pourri.

It's a Gift

There are times when employees voluntarily give presents to their coworkers, such as for birthdays or during the holidays. However, one assemblage of office idiots has an entirely different mindset when it comes to gifts—especially the receiving of gifts. Take the case of the help-desk technician in your company who repairs your computer, and then expects you to give her a gift, such as a discount card for a restaurant or online store. You offer her nothing but thanks, and now you're finding that she's very slow to get around to your requests.

Clearly, employees shouldn't be requiring gifts for doing their job, nor should they be accepting gifts that are offered in this context. While such offerings can be called gifts, the more accurate label is a "bribe." The message is that unless you go along with this program, your computer programs will suffer.

One strategy is to approach this person and tell her that you're concerned about the appropriateness and ethics of her expectations. The only problem is that you're not likely to get far with this line of reasoning. After all, she has apparently faced no repercussions as a result of her "present" behavior, and she senses no reason to shut off the faucet of required beneficence. Besides, she probably would not set aside time to meet with you in the first place unless you were bearing gifts.

You're better off discussing this matter with her manager. And unless this manager is somehow part of the "gifted program," he or she is likely to take prompt corrective action. All you'd need to say is, "What's the department's policy regarding gifts in exchange for work performed by members of your team?" The most likely response will be, "What?" And then you should simply let the facts tell the rest of the story. Soon enough, this combo platter of gifts and graft will be history. And the same fate just might befall the employee who's behind it.

Money Talks

The issue of money is fully vested in a vast array of totally idiotic workplace behaviors. One of the most common and egregious examples is the tendency of some employees to brag about their salaries and finances, all in complete disregard of the needs, interests, and economic condition of their audience. In the trade, this is known as counting your money in public, and it's far more of a liability than an asset.

Take the situation in which your boss loves to brag about his money and possessions, to the point of showing you photos of what he just bought or what he plans to buy. All of you put up with this braggadocio because you need your jobs, but his obsession with his opulence is becoming increasingly difficult to stomach. One question immediately comes to mind is, who's your manager trying to impress? Most employees are not dazzled by excessive displays of personal wealth by their higher-ups. So he must be trying to impress himself. If he were succeeding, the boasting would stop.

The most common employee reactions to such idiocy include annoyance, resentment, boredom, and even a tinge of pity. Yes, employees can actually feel sorry for a wealthy manager who has so much insecurity and so little going on in his life that he must resort to flashing his money and possessions to make himself feel good or more powerful. When he descends into show-and-tell mode, you and your coworkers may be cornered and feel obligated to sit through these displays and feign polite interest. Unfortunately, obsequious comments that indicate even mild interest will only set the stage for repeat performances.

—————————————————

You basically have two ways to deal with this type of situation. One strategy is for you and a few of your fellow employees to have a face-to-face conversation with your manager regarding his possession obsession. However, this approach implies that you have a decent working relationship with him, one that includes truly open, two-way communication. The problem is that managers who engage in showy behavior don't typically show much receptiveness to input from their employees.

Nonetheless, if you believe that your relationship with him is strong enough to sail into these potentially perilous waters, you'd meet with him and at some point say, "I really don't think you want to hurt us, insult us, or make us feel bad about ourselves," and then stop and look at him. He would have no choice but to agree and say something like, "No, I don't want to do that at all." At that point, he'll probably ask what he could possibly be doing to cause any of you to feel this way. You'd then say, "We're not in the same financial position as you, and although we're happy that you've got money and so many cool things, it makes us feel kind of bad about ourselves." This is basically playing the guilt card and making him feel badly about what he's doing. In fact, this is playing the card so strongly that even the most idiotic manager is likely to get it. The result is that you're likely to see fewer displays of flash and cash after this type of exchange. The unspoken message associated with this approach, of course, is that if a manager's actions are causing the employees to feel hurt, that can't be good for motivation, morale, productivity, or loyalty. Unless your manager's skin is thicker than his wallet, he'll get this message as well.

There's also a safer approach. The next time you're corralled for one of his opulence episodes, look for a break in the action and then excuse yourself because of pressing job demands, saying something like, "I'm sorry, but I promised so-and-so I'd get back to him right now," or "Oh, sorry, I'm going to fall behind on the such-and-such project if I don't jump on it, so if you don't mind, I have to run." By opening with an apology, you immediately block him from thinking that you're being rude or impolite. The apologetic opening also serves as an initial attention-grabber that will focus his attention on the comments that follow—namely, the fact that you're hitting the exit ramp. The more that you and your associates remove yourselves from these follies, the less motivated he'll be to share his portfolios with you. After all, when it comes to show-and-tell, if there's no one to show, there's no need to tell.

What's Yours is Theirs

Some of the more unique displays of office idiocy originate from thought patterns that are not only out to lunch, but out to breakfast and dinner, as well. It's as if hordes of office idiots have dedicated themselves to concocting the most ludicrous workplace behaviors, followed by even more nonsensical explanations and rationalizations for them. One of the more bizarre iterations of such idiocy is centered on some of the most basic elements in any workplace, the supplies and equipment. But not just any supplies and equipment. Your supplies and equipment.

Take the case in which your job requires you to be away from your workstation several times a day. In the world of rational workplace behavior, this isn't a problem. But in the world of office idiocy, this poses a unique opportunity for absurdity. When you're away, a coworker from an adjacent workstation steps in. Why? She has run short of supplies—pens, notepads, a stapler. So she takes yours. Of course, when you return and end up needing any of those items, you end up wasting time rifling through drawers in a futile effort to find them.

In and of itself, your coworker's tendency to habitually and unilaterally help herself to your office supplies reeks of office idiocy. But wait, there's more! Her explanation is the capper. When you ask her to please refrain from taking your supplies, her response is, "They're not really yours. They belong to the company, and that's all of us. So I can take what I want when I want it." Your first response is likely to be something along the lines of, "Huh?"

This is followed by the instantaneous realization that you're now face-to-face with a certifiable office idiot. Using her loopy logic, she not only has a right to your supplies, but she can just as easily waltz in and take your phone, your computer, your chair, or your desk. What she fails to realize is the obvious fact that although the items she has been taking are indeed company property, they're assigned to you in the context of your job. This is all the ownership you need. If she would like to use these items, she needs to ask for your permission. In fact, she shouldn't even be *entering* your workstation unless she has your permission.

Unfortunately, if you present this explanation to her, she's likely to say that you just don't understand. So, rather than trying to explain anything to her, you should simply say, "Look, when things are taken out of my workstation, I end up wasting time hunting for them. The solution is for you to please stay out of my workstation unless I'm there or have given you permission. You can do that, can't you?" You're giving her a fairly direct command by saying "You can do that," and you're setting her up to reflexively say yes to the question that follows. And if you get anything but a yes, you'd say something like, "Well, if this continues, I'm going to have to talk to our manager about it."

If she keeps on treating your workstation like her personal supply cabinet, your next stop is indeed your manager's office. When you get there, start with the facts of this little episode. Once they're on the table, let your manager see how this idiocy can work its way into his life, such as by saying, "You know, since she thinks she can stroll into my workstation and take whatever she wants, she probably thinks that she can do this anywhere in the company. Maybe your office. Maybe the president's."

By putting your manager on notice that an avaricious office idiot is on the loose, your manager will be more likely to take action, rather than wait for the president's chair to go missing.

Family Connections

Family businesses are the backbone of the American economy. In fact, the majority of businesses in America are family businesses, and they're the source of more than 50 percent of all paid wages. While family businesses are fertile ground for planting and growing visionary, enterprising, and entrepreneurial businesspeople, they're also fertile ground for harvesting office idiots. Most of the problems encountered in a family business are derived from one common source: focusing more on family than business. When the organization chart looks like a family tree, or when a company meeting looks like a family reunion, the stage is set for family matters to trump business matters.

Let's say you're working in a family business, but it's not your family. The owner has hired a couple of his children, a few nieces and nephews, and a sprinkling of in-laws, as well. One of his nephews is a college student who interned in your department over the summer. You gave him a range of projects, and he half-heartedly went through the motions of working on them. To put it nicely, you found him to score high in such areas as arrogance, sense of entitlement, and smugness.

Now that the summer and internship have come to an end, this nephew has been contacting you for advice on a paper that he apparently needs to write in order to receive credit for interning. He keeps asking you for more and more information, and he sends you sections of the paper for you to read, edit, and even rewrite. You're not exactly delighted with this activity, but you're not sure how to handle it, especially since the owner thinks his nephew can do no wrong.

A summer internship is often part of a college program in which students receive credit for the learning experience that emanates from interning. Since your indulged intern is incessantly bombarding you with questions, the real question is whether he learned anything at all. Either way, there's a collegiate lesson that he apparently has not learned, namely, the fact that the university requires him to do his own work and write his own papers from start to finish. It's not only an intrusion and interruption for you to spend any time on his paper, it's also an ethical violation for you to write one word of it.

■———————————————

Rather than being a reluctant ghostwriter, you should tell this former intern that you've gone as far as you can go on this assignment, and he needs to finish this paper on his own. If he does anything but agree, your next step is to meet with the owner and put an end to this charade. The best strategy for doing so is to avoid lambasting or labeling the nephew, as such an approach is guaranteed to generate a harsh reaction from his protective uncle. Rather, you should present the facts of the situation, especially in terms of this nephew's expectation that you're to play a role in writing and editing of this paper. Once the facts are laid out, say something like, "I'm very concerned that your nephew is violating university rules by asking me to do all this writing and editing for him. Colleges expel students for this type of thing, and I think he's setting himself up for a real problem. He's got more than enough data to write a good paper, and that's what he should do. It'd be a great learning experience for him." At that point, stop talking and wait for the owner's response.

His reaction will be a most interesting learning experience for you.

Are You Busy?

There's a gaggle of office idiots who fly solo and occasionally in flocks, seemingly with but one mission in mind: to drop by and visit their fellow employees. They simply appear in your office or cubicle—individually or with a buddy or two—and there's no notice, warning, or appointment; you look up, and there they are. Perhaps they're looking for information. Perhaps they're looking to spill information. Perhaps they just want to socialize. Regardless, as soon as they're within range, their typical first words form one of the most idiotic inquiries that can be proffered in any organization: "Are you busy?"

How should you respond? If you say yes, you come across as inaccessible, unapproachable, and somewhat nasty. If you say no, it sounds as though you don't have enough to do. Although it may be tempting to respond with "Of course I'm busy!" such a response isn't likely to do much for one's warm-and-fuzzy rating. So, when one or more of these office idiots lands in your office or workstation and in-quires as to the status of your activity level, you should say, "Sure, I'm busy, but what's up?" With this approach, you're politely letting them know that you are indeed busy, while clearly implying this isn't a great time for an interruption unless it's an emergency. By definition, the terse question, "What's up?" calls for an equally terse response. It's far less inviting than saying, for example, "What's going on?" or "What's cooking?" both of which instantly open your door for extended visit-ing hours.

———————————————————————————————■

Unfortunately, many office idiots are not masters at picking up cues. If there's a chair, they'll sit. If there's a wall, they'll lean. If there's a desk, they'll perch. They have no qualms about feeling at home in your office, in spite of your subtle messages to the contrary. Take the situation where one of these itinerant idiots has popped into your office and plopped into a chair. You've already said you're busy, and you've played the "What's up?" card, all to no avail. She's comfortably ensconced across from you, and she's ready to talk. About nothing.

■———————————————————————————————

When literally faced with this office idiot, a little assertiveness can go a long way. And it can induce this coworker to go a long way, too. One of the easiest and most effective comments to pry her out of this comfort zone is for you to quickly say, "I'm sorry, but this just isn't a good time to talk. I've got all sorts of major stuff to get done, and I'm on a tight deadline. Let me get back to you after I wrap things up." After this, you simply stop talking. Notice that your comments are not critical or condescending, and they're focused on you and your workload, not on your uninvited guest. You use the words "I" and "me" five times, while saying "you" only once. And further, you're framing your comments in a warm and self-deprecating context by opening with an apology, a strategy that makes your comments more palatable. Because a good number of drop-in idiots are likely to straggle back to your landing pad in spite of an initial spurning, the last sentence clearly advises your visitor to refrain from another drop-in until you've contacted her.

The final piece of business in dealing with these interruptions is to apply the power of nonverbal communication. When an uninvited office idiot pops into your office and appears ready to plop into a chair, stand up. When you're standing, a visitor is far less likely to sit down. And if you deliver the comments noted above while you're standing, their impact will be even stronger.

The bottom line is that you should literally stand for these interruptions, especially if you figuratively can't stand them.

Me First

No matter how long you've been working with, for, over, under, around, or in spite of office idiots, there'll still be times when their actions and antics are going to stun you. If you think about it, at this very moment in companies all around the world, there are office idiots engaging in behaviors that are so shockingly outrageous, ridiculous, and absurd that they would never even cross your mind. You'll know that you're encountering one of these idiotic phenomena if you find yourself standing there with mouth agape.

You never really know when such idiocy is going to jump onto your radar screen. Sometimes it's associated with a complex business matter, and other times it emanates from the most basic of workplace issues. For example, take the resoundingly mundane situation of your desk chair breaking. Your company has a simple procedure to deal with this. Namely, you let your manager know, and she'll have Facilities order a new chair. You follow these steps, and the order for a new chair is officially in the works. So far, so good. But when the chair arrives, so does the idiocy. As the final pieces of protective plastic are peeled away, your manager grabs the chair and gives you her old one.

Who in the world would even think to do such a thing? No one, other than an office idiot.

Before you roll into action (in her old chair), step back and take a careful look at your manager. She's an office idiot whose behavior in this instance tells everyone that she's tough, uncaring, self-serving, self-centered, and selfish. These are not the qualities of a manager who's likely to listen to your persuasive comments and say, "You're right. What was I thinking? I'm so sorry. Here—please take the chair."

There's no question that your manager's idiotic behavior here raises questions about her insight, sensitivity, and concern for the members of her team. After all, when it comes to chairs—and apparently a lot more—she clearly has some "deep-seated" issues. However, if you think about the possible outcomes associated with confronting her, not one of them has a happy ending. If you somehow prevail and end up with the new chair, she's going to be annoyed every time she sits in her old chair. And guess who will be the target of her annoyance?

If she refuses to give up the new chair, she's likely to be upset that you asked her to do that and put her in an awkward and embarrassing position. And guess again as to who will be the target of her annoyance? In other words, this is a lose-lose situation for you. Plus, this isn't the most serious matter in the world. It's just a chair. This means that you need to pick your battles. Is it worth getting into a fracas with your manager over this, especially if there's no way for you to come out on top? Nope.

When a more serious and significant issue occurs with this office idiot, one that doesn't fall into the realm of a guaranteed lose-lose outcome, you should jump out of her old chair and stand up to her. But until then, the best way to deal with this type of office idiocy is to sit it out. Literally.

15

HOW TO AVOID BECOMING
AN OFFICE IDIOT

Many studies today are finding that one of the most powerful strategies to foster effective performance, successful outcomes, and goal attainment is the use of a checklist. Such a list would include every key action you need to take in order to be absolutely certain that the work you're performing includes all of the critical steps, functions and benchmarks necessary for a positive outcome, while simultaneously remaining free of omissions, oversights, and lapses.

With your trusty checklist in hand as you engage in any significant activity, the idea is to make sure that every item is checked off as you proceed, thereby guaranteeing that you're taking all of the right steps, and doing so at the right time. It doesn't matter if you're piloting a plane, removing a spleen, taking a trip, playing a sport, or planting a tree, a checklist is going to help you literally and figuratively get where you want to go, and make this journey correctly, safely, and successfully.

With this mind, if one of your goals is to avoid becoming an office idiot, here's a checklist that will help keep any idiotic tendencies in check:

☐ **Place a real value on learning.** The world is changing, and one of the easiest ways to become an office idiot is to fall behind by failing to change with it. The antidote for this condition is to make sure that you read the latest articles in your field, network with sharp people, take online and offline classes, attend seminars, and stay current on current events.

☐ **Practice active listening.** When communicating with others, try to rephrase, reframe, and even repeat what they're saying. This will not only help you understand their message, but will also signal that you're actively engaged, interested, and involved in what they're saying.

☐ **Keep your e-mail businesslike.** If you find that an e-mail exchange is turning into an argument or filling up with emotions, end it immediately and either pick up your phone or pick up your feet and handle the matter offline.

☐ **Manage your time.** Make sure that you're handling your top priorities first, using your most productive hours to handle your most demanding work, and regularly monitoring your work to be sure that your current project is making the best use of your time—and if it's not, switch to a project that makes more sense.

☐ **Walk the ethical walk.** Instead of making grandiose pronouncements about the importance of ethical behavior at work, let your actions do the talking. And in case you're wondering if a particular action would be ethical, just ask yourself how you'd feel it went viral and had two million hits before you even had breakfast.

☐ **Maintain positive expectations.** If you expect positive outcomes, whether in dealings with your manager, your peers, or your subordinates, you're more likely to engage in behaviors that actually bring out the favorable results that you seek. And conversely, if you have negative expectations regarding your dealings with others at work, you'll automatically increase the likelihood of less-than-favorable outcomes.

☐ **Focus your feedback on performance not personality.** If you want your constructive criticism to be heard, focus on performance, outcomes, behaviors, and results. Stay away from labeling, personal comments, and remarks that center on the recipient's personality or character traits. And by the way, it's far better to give negative feedback in private, and positive feedback in public.

☐ **Remember the importance of nonverbal communication.** Note the fact that when you interact with others, approximately 80 percent of any message is nonverbal. As a result, you may have all of the right information and words, but your tone, tenor, and body language can send a totally different message. Overlooking the role of nonverbal communication easily turns any message into an idiotic mess.

☐ **Manage by wandering around.** If you're in management, get out of your office frequently and take a look at what's going on in your department and beyond. And when you do so, concentrate on using all of your senses. You can learn a great deal by looking around, listening carefully, touching the materials, and sniffing the air. By the way, it's better for your health for you to get up and walk around than it is to sit at your desk for countless hours.

☐ **Practice pre-hire professionalism.** When you conduct a job interview, keep all of your questions job-related and focus on the applicant's work history and expertise. And be sure to do more listening than talking. If *you're* the job candidate, be sure to read about the company in advance, get to the interview at least 10 minutes early, keep your answers clear and to the point, have some good questions of your own, pay close attention to the interviewer's body language, and write a follow-up e-mail thanking the interviewer for his or her time.

☐ **Stop stereotyping.** Biases and stereotypes are quite prevalent among the ranks of office idiots everywhere. Rather than joining those ranks, do whatever you can to make sure that their archaic and mean-spirited misconceptions play no role in your organization. After all, there's no question that diversity enriches every aspect of an organization's ability to create, adapt, perform, and thrive.

☐ **Vary your leadership style.** Don't waste time looking for the Holy Grail of leadership, namely the one best way to lead. There isn't one. Leadership is a situational process, and there'll be times when you need to be firm and direct, as well as times when you can turn an entire decision over to your employees. Take a careful look at the time constraints, magnitude of the decision, resources required, and the knowledge, skills, and abilities of your employees, and then adjust your leadership style accordingly.

☐ **Treat others with respect and trust.** By integrating respect and trust into your style as a leader, you automatically engage in such non-idiotic behaviors as understanding your employees as individuals, listening to them, demonstrating sympathy and empathy, responding to their queries and concerns, doing more empowering than controlling, soliciting ideas and input, setting realistic expectations, recognizing accomplishments, and providing opportunities to learn, achieve, grow, and advance.

☐ **Be social media savvy.** If you haven't done so already, enter the world of social media by using such services as Facebook, LinkedIn, Twitter, Google+, Instagram, Yammer, and Chatter in your work. These are powerful resources for external and internal networking, all with proven success in enhancing communication and collaboration, as well as taking marketing and customer service to entirely new levels. Your coworkers and competition are most likely on board, and you'll be left behind if you don't join them.

☐ **Establish realistic goals.** When it comes to setting goals, regardless of whether you've established them for yourself or in conjunction with your manager or your employees, they've got to be realistic. If goals are so simple that you can reach them in your sleep, they're useless; if they're so demanding that they're beyond your grasp, they're just as useless. And no matter what your goals may be, they'll need to be backed up with specific action plans that spell out priorities, benchmarks along the way, deadlines, and measurement strategies.

☐ **Work by the Golden Rule.** And finally, the best way to avoid being an office idiot is to use the Golden Rule as your guide. The idea is to treat everyone in your workplace just as you'd like to be treated. By considering this rule in dealings with your manager, your fellow employees, your subordinates, and anyone else who comes into contact with you and your organization, the likelihood of engaging in idiotic behaviors is all but eliminated.

INDEX

ABOUT THE AUTHOR

Ken Lloyd, PhD, is a nationally recognized management consultant, author, speaker, and newspaper columnist. His weekly workplace advice column runs in several newspapers, including the *Los Angeles Daily News* and others that are part of the Los Angeles Newspaper Group.

Over the years, Dr. Lloyd has taught numerous MBA classes on communication, leadership, and organizational behavior at The Anderson School at UCLA. He also serves as vice president of planning and development at Strategic Partners, Inc., and has lectured at many universities. He is frequently sought as a guest speaker at meetings, conferences, and other business gatherings. He has appeared on *Good Morning America*, CNN, *Morning Edition* on NPR, plus frequent appearances on KABC, KTLA, and Fox Morning News *Ask the Expert* segments. He is a graduate of UC–Berkeley, and he received his MS and PhD in organizational behavior from UCLA. He is a member of the American Psychological Association and the Society for Industrial and Organizational Psychology.

Dr. Lloyd has authored and coauthored several successful books, his most recent being *Performance Appraisals and Phrases for Dummies* (Wiley: *For Dummies,* September, 2009). He is also the author of *Jerks at Work: How to Deal With People Problems and Problem People* (Career Press, 1999; revised edition, 2006), *151 Quick Ideas to Recognize and Reward Employees* (Career Press, 2007), *Be the Boss Your Employees Deserve* (Career Press, 2002), and *The K.I.S.S. Guide to Selling* (Dorling Kindersley, 2001). In addition, he co-authored (with Dr. Donald Moine) *Ultimate Selling Power: How to Create and Enjoy a Multimillion Dollar Sales Career* (Career Press, 2002) and *Unlimited Selling Power: How to Master Hypnotic Selling Skills* (Prentice Hall, 1990). He is also the author of the business film, *Communication: The Name of the Game*, which was an award winner at the National Educational Film Festival and the American Film Festival (Roundtable Films and Video). His books have been translated into more than a dozen languages and are sold around the world.

You can contact Dr. Lloyd at his Website: *www.jerksatwork.com*.